THE POWE

`You HAS NEVER BEEN

CALCULATED!!

REFUSE TO LOSE :)

THE POWER INSIDE OF
YOU HAS NEVER BEEN
CALCULATED !!

REFUSE TO LOSE

7 STEPS TO MAKE ADVERSITY YOUR ADVANTAGE

ADELL J. HARRIS

LIONCREST
PUBLISHING

REFUSE TO LOSE

7 Steps to Make Adversity Your Advantage

ISBN   978-1-5445-0263-2 *Hardcover*

978-1-5445-0261-8 *Paperback*

978-1-5445-0262-5 *Ebook*

To my mother, Joretta Allen Harris—your spirit lives in my work, and my love for you grows stronger every day.

*To the reader, the time for transformation is **now**!*

CONTENTS

INTRODUCTION

Throughout my life, I have faced adversity. I've experienced pain, loss, and trauma. At times, my pain threatened to define not only my life but who I was as a person. But, by following the steps I outline in this book, I was able to embrace my adversity and rewrite my story.

MY STORY

Let's begin at the end. It was June 6, and the year was 2014. It was a hot day in my hometown of High Point, North Carolina, also known as the furniture capital of the world and home to about 100,000. I was standing in my mother's bedroom, in the childhood home I'd been raised in. The windows were open but creating zero breeze. Sweat poured down my back and my face as I tossed completely full, ninety-gallon-sized trash bags out her second-floor window, bag after bag. I was alone. I was exhausted. I was angry. I was sad. With every toss, my emotions grew stronger and stronger. This was the hardest thing I'd ever experienced.

Earlier that day, we'd celebrated my mother's sixty-two years of life and laid her physical body to rest. Just four days prior, the woman who knew and loved me first, Joretta Allen Harris, had lost her battle with diabetes. I was overwhelmed with emotion and grief. I was also caught off guard by all the responsibility that death leaves for the closest of kin. I selected the last dress that she would wear, the casket that would encase her body, and the words for her obituary, and now, I was cleaning out every inch of the house that she'd lived in for thirty-plus years. It had been a long four days. It had actually been a long two and a half years, as my mother had lived her final years in poor health.

I had been going one hundred miles per hour, taking care of this and that. The intensity of the moment was coming to a head. Tears began to well up as I rested my hands on my knees, as a tired athlete does. I began to speak out loud.

"Where are all the people who lived here? Where is my brother? How am I here by myself?"

After my brief pity party, I asked a question that changed my life: "What is this here to teach me?"

I then began to open myself up to the benefits of the moment. *Of everyone who could be doing this, why not me?* I thought. Maybe I needed to be the one cleaning out this house, standing in my mother's bedroom, throwing bags of trash out the window. It was symbolic. This was the end—of so many things. This was the end of hospital rooms, nursing homes, dialysis, and sickness. This was the end of physical moments with my mom. This was the end of the pain, hate, and anger that I associated with this house. Acknowledging this allowed me to release these emotions, which brought me a sense of peace. This experience was intense, and I knew I never would've done it willingly. I wouldn't have found myself in that house in that situation if circumstances hadn't forced me there, but *I was supposed to be there.* By cleaning out that house, I was cleansing my spirit, too.

I was adopted at three months old, and my adoptive parents divorced when I was three. My adoptive father largely dropped out of my life at that point. He always paid his child support, and I did see him occasionally on holidays and special occasions, but he didn't play the role of loving, present father. Today, I have no relationship with him. I don't think he meant to hurt me in the ways he did. I believe that he, like everyone in this world, was doing the best he could. But fatherless children live a different reality, and his absence has irrefutably changed my life.

My adoptive mother was tough, the epitome of an alpha woman. She had good intentions with everyone she met. She was a helper that gave more than she got. Like a lot of parents in the '80s, she led using fear and had no problem dropping the hammer. I know my mother loved me, but growing up, it was hard for me to understand it. Love can be complex. She constantly pointed out my shortcomings, flaws, and faults. My hair wasn't done. I smelled bad. I ran my mouth too much. My teeth were yellow. I struggled in math. I dressed sloppy. I wasn't as smart as my brother. Her delivery was aggressive and sometimes physical. I interpreted this to mean that I wasn't good enough. She probably thought she was being helpful, showing me the things I could improve on. She never taught me how to do these things differently, though, so she came across as a bully. Her disapproval affected my self-image and confidence. I desperately wanted her approval and love.

She had to be both father and mother to me, and perhaps I expected even more of her because of that. With being adopted, having no father, and feeling unloved, I was constantly seeking attention. Children want to feel loved by their parents. I was no different.

My mother remarried four times after my father, but none of those men were father figures. My mother was very religious, and she always told me that having sex before marriage was a sin. So, if she was going to have sex with a man, she had to marry him first. This is how people use religion to support their dysfunctional behavior. Five husbands, no fathers? This ratio would eventually have a negative impact on our relationship.

My mother's second husband was an evil and disgusting human being. I don't use those words lightly. He used to beat my brother and me with extension cords, usually for forgetting to add "sir" or "ma'am" to the end of a response. Beyond the strict rules and discipline, his presence changed my life forever when he decided to touch me inappropriately and expose himself during one of my evening baths. He never should have been in our home in the first place. He and my mother had separated, but she allowed him to continue living with us for a short time. He moved out of her bedroom to a bedroom across the hall from mine, which meant he and I began sharing a bathroom. I was eight years old with a secret.

Throughout my childhood, starting when I was nine, my mother fostered dozens of kids—at least fifty. Our house was filled with young people separated from their families, kids all too familiar with pain, disappointment, rejection, abuse, anger, and sadness. The first five kids became like family to me. I called them my brothers and sisters, and they lived with us until they were eighteen. Once they phased out of the system, I never saw them again. One day they were my sister or brother, and the next, they were out of our house and out of my life forever. This was when I began to build protective walls in my relationships, as I realized that if I never got close to people, I couldn't be affected by their departure.

Early on, my mother would foster one child, then two, then three, four, and five. By the time I was in high school, our house began to feel less like a foster home and more like a group home, with as many as five to eight young boys at any given time. My mom would take in anyone, including those who acted out or who had been kicked out of other foster homes. Just like me, these kids had their own sadness, trauma, and toxic behaviors. I grew immune to the process, and in my last three years at home, every new child was a stranger; I had no desire to build any new relationships. My mother worked two jobs and was hardly home. I was greatly outnumbered with no one to protect my space or me. I remember having to buy an exterior lock for my bedroom door to protect my things while I wasn't home. My things were still stolen. This too would cause a divide in my relationship with my mother.

My childhood home haunted me—not because of drug use or alcohol abuse or domestic violence, but because of the sexual dysfunction that every person that lived in that home experienced. From my sexual abuse at eight years old, to the regularity of pornographic magazines and sexually explicit letters from my mom's incarcerated pen pal lying around the house, to teenage girls having babies by teenage boys as a result of sexual relationships that started in our home—it was a house of secrets. Everyone in my home was hurting, looking for love, wanting to feel needed and important.

Life outside my home came with its own challenges. When I was in high school in the mid-nineties, there was a rise in drug use across the country, known as the crack epidemic. High Point, like a lot of America's cities, was impacted. During my high school years, violent crime in High Point reached record numbers. Thanks to my tough single mother, I was shielded from much of the drug use and violence. I'm grateful that she worked so hard, putting in sixty or more hours a week so that we could keep our house on the north end of town where violent crime wasn't as prevalent. She and my father had purchased that house together, expecting to have two incomes to make the mortgage payments, but she managed to make ends meet all by herself.

Still, despite our fairly safe neighborhood that was for the most part free of drugs, I did not escape the growing toxicity unscathed. In my senior year, one of my classmates was killed by a stray bullet just twenty-five yards from me. Within that same year, my best friend committed suicide.

I left for Wake Forest University on a basketball scholarship with all of this trauma and pain bottled up inside of me, festering in a dark corner of my mind. I struggled with depression, anxiety, and suicidal thoughts throughout college. I spent endless energy being furious at my mother and father for all the things that had happened to me in my childhood. I felt the intensity of my past in every moment.

Shortly after I graduated, my first love, my grandmother, passed away from lung cancer. This was about all I could take. She had been my rock my entire life. I always say that she was the first person to love me unconditionally. I didn't have to be the best student, best basketball player, have my hair done, or dress nice to receive her love. The pain of losing her sent me into a downward spiral of harmful behavior and alcoholism.

My personal life was in shambles, but as I always had, I was able to hide behind my basketball success. It was no longer as a player but as a college coach. Actor Terry Crews once said, "Success gives us a warm place to hide." I get that, because I lived it. I was working as an assistant coach, and I was enjoying success in my role. However, alcohol was vastly becoming more of my identity. I was a binge drinker. I never had just one or two drinks; instead of one shot, I'd have six, and instead of a couple of beers, I'd have a dozen.

My downward spiral ended with being arrested for driving the wrong way down a one-way street with a blood alcohol concentration almost three times the legal limit.

My DUI was a turning point. I had let my pain control me and my actions for far too long, and *something* needed to change. I couldn't go on living the way I had. I needed to find a way to handle and process my past adversities, and that's exactly what I set out to do. I'd already been studying personal development and highly successful people for nearly seven years at this point. That work had allowed me to survive, holding on by my fingertips, but I was done just surviving. I wanted to *thrive*.

I decided that a move was necessary; I resigned from my assistant coach position at UNC Asheville and contacted the athletic director at Tusculum College about the vacant head coaching position. I was hired as the head coach at Tusculum College in May 2009, just three months after my DUI. It was a new beginning birthed out of adversity. I slowly began to realize that my cracks and wounds did not make me broken. They made me unstoppable. This was the realization I had on that hot summer day in June. As I embraced my adversity, new cycles of growth and opportunity arose, which eventually led me to walk away from my fourteen-year coaching career and create Refuse to Lose LLC, a personal empowerment company created to inspire the world to make adversity their advantage.

THE PROBLEM: UNTREATED ADVERSITY

After reading my story, you might think you have nothing in common with me. However, I believe you and I aren't all that different. We all spend so much time and energy trying to avoid pain, but nobody makes it through life unscathed, free of scars. Pain is inevitable—the cost of admission to being human. We are all living the human experience where we are disappointed, where we make mistakes and fail, where people do us wrong, where we suffer injustice and oppression, where we face lack and limitation.

I don't know what your specific struggles are or what challenges you've faced. Maybe you've been fired from your job or don't have enough money to make ends meet. Perhaps you've been bullied or told you're not good enough. Maybe you've been sexually abused, or perhaps you've had your heart broken or lost a loved one.

Some pain is acute, lasting only a few days or weeks, and some is chronic, lasting years or even your whole life if you don't properly address it. But no matter what your specific situation is, pain is pain. Your struggles and hurts are valid, no matter how small or inconsequential they may seem. We're all different, with different stories, but we are connected in our journey by the unifying, universal emotion of pain.

Pain itself is not the issue, though. Without darkness, there would be no light, and without pain, we would not fully appreciate the goodness in our lives. As unbelievable as it may sound, pain can be a gift. The adversities we face—our stresses and traumas, our hurts and wounds—can be an advantage. However, the effect adversity has on our lives depends entirely upon how we react to, process, and live with it.

Though we all experience pain, we respond to it differently, often in unhealthy ways. Some people bottle up their pain inside and try to pretend it doesn't exist, until one day it erupts, and they can ignore it no longer. Some people try to mask it, turning to drugs or food or promiscuous behaviors. Other people lash out, becoming the source of hate, bigotry, and prejudice—creating a negative ripple effect in the world. Still other people lose hope and fall into depression, unable to move forward, paralyzed.

From the micro to the macro, you *need* to deal with your pain. If you don't treat a wound, it becomes infected. Emotional and psychological wounds are no different. Untreated, they fester and rot. At best, untreated trauma and stress will prevent you from moving forward and building the life you really want to live. At worst, it could literally kill you.

I believe unattended adversity is the number-one cause of death in our country. Obesity, opioid abuse, alcohol addiction, violence against others or ourselves, crime—these are all ways in which untreated pain manifests, and these are all killers. More than a third of the American population now suffers from obesity, and in the next decade, more people will die from diabetes than ever before. Every single day people die from drug overdoses, suicide, and violence, and a staggering number of incarcerated women—some studies estimate between 47 and 82 percent—were victims of childhood sexual abuse. Other studies say 94 percent of incarcerated women have been victimized sexually, some as children, others as adults.[1] It's no coincidence that women who have suffered such deep pain would end up locked behind bars. Pain can send people down dangerous paths.

You cannot allow your pain to control you. You cannot let yourself be held back from achieving your full potential. You must refuse to lose.

THE SOLUTION: REFUSE TO LOSE

When you refuse to lose, you make the decision that *you will be okay* after the storm has passed, after you have

---

1   Chandra Bozelko, "Sexual Abuse Survivors Deserve Help, Not Punishment," *Huffpost*, February 18, 2018, https://www.huffingtonpost.com/entry/opinion-bozelko-sexual-abuse-prison_us_5a871e17e4b00bc49f43c39a.

made it through whatever difficulties you are facing. Deep within, you decide, *I will not lose. No matter what. My pain will not define me. It is one part of my journey, but it's not going to be the biggest portion. I have a whole marathon left to live, and I'm going to come out stronger and better than ever.*

The key to achieving this mentality is finding something greater than your pain. For me, this was my faith and the sport of basketball, and all the people I met and grew to love because of those two things.

We all have something within us that wants and desires more—some inner drive that pushes us to find meaning in our lives. We all have a purpose, a reason for being on this earth. I believe our job is to find out what our purpose is—how we can make use of our inherited talents and gifts, our unique oneness, to give back to the world. In doing this, our purpose can replace pain as the dominating force in our lives, guiding us through any storm.

In both fiction and real life—from Rocky Balboa to Oprah Winfrey—we have been given countless examples of people who have adopted the refuse-to-lose mindset. After not believing in themselves, after rejection, after insecurities, after deep and suffocating pain, these people chose to become the heroes of their own stories and, in so doing, made the world a better place for those who came behind them.

The refuse-to-lose mindset is based on seven simple steps:

1. Acknowledge your pain.
2. Accept your pain.
3. Rewrite your story.
4. Model the attitudes and behaviors you desire.
5. Take your E (empathy) and G (gratitude) vitamins.
6. State your cause.
7. Share your story.

When you follow these steps, you make adversity your advantage. You don't "overcome" your pain; you own it and use it. We are creatures born for expansion and growth. We are the greatest form of creation, and all of us know that there is more to our lives—even if that knowledge is buried deep inside or shoved into the corner of our minds.

Though we were built for growth, we tend to find our bubbles of comfort, and then we stagnate, thinking, *This is good enough.* In the depths of adversity, though, no one ever thinks, *This is good enough.* Instead, when we face deep pain, we are filled with the certainty that *there must be more.*

Adversity opens us to resourcefulness and curiosity. It

is the birthplace of innovation. I've never been content and have always been obsessed with growth, but where I focus my learning changes based on how well I know myself and where I am in my journey. Each day, I continue to learn who I am. It's like that old saying: "You don't know what you don't know."

Adversity forces you to change, and you get to choose whether you will grow into a new, better version of yourself or fall into toxic attitudes and behaviors. While I, of course, would not wish pain on anyone, your pain is a deep well of energy that you can use to transform yourself and your life. When you begin to look at adversity through this empowering lens, you will unlock unlimited potential.

This is not to say that your pain shouldn't hurt or be uncomfortable. Frequently in my sports career, when I faced physical pain and exhaustion, I would tell myself, "Suck it up. You're tougher than that." Later, as a coach, I would tell my players the exact same thing. So much of the time, we're not given permission to feel our pain. The refuse-to-lose mentality isn't about "sucking it up." Acknowledging and experiencing your hurt is important, but eventually, it will be time to ask yourself, *Now what am I going to do with this pain?* I believe the only acceptable answer is, *I'm going to turn it into something incredible that would have never existed otherwise.*

To free yourself from the prison of adversity, you have to work on yourself every single day. The process described in this book isn't a one-time fix; it's a lifestyle. If you want to be the best version of yourself, if you want to live with full freedom, unshackled by pain, if you want to own your outcome, you must live the refuse-to-lose mindset every single day.

For years, we go to school, sit in classrooms, and take notes. We are overloaded with knowledge and forced to grow. Then, we get out of school, and there's nothing to challenge us—nothing to strengthen who we are, how we think, or how we feel. No one is forcing you to grow any-more, so *you* have to make the decision for yourself. You can lie wounded, or you can pick yourself up and march into battle, wearing your scars proudly. It's your choice.

WHAT THIS BOOK OFFERS YOU

I know firsthand how destructive adversity can be if it goes untreated. I watched my mother die because of untreated adversity, I lost my best friend because of it, and I nearly took my own life because of it. Worse, I put others' lives in danger with my drunk driving. I truly believe this can be a life-or-death choice: make adver-sity your advantage or continue to let pain control you.

Of course, sometimes it's not a question of life or death;

sometimes it's about making the most of the time you have here on earth and taking full advantage of the opportunities available to you. It's about deciding that "good enough" isn't actually enough.

No matter who you are, no matter what adversity or stress you've faced in your life, adopting the refuse-to-lose mindset will help you make adversity your advantage and reach your full potential.

I've pursued a lot of study, reflection, and behavior modification to create a different path for myself. I've read countless books, watched endless interviews, and investigated every aspect of my role models' lives and behavior. I've studied human behavior, leadership, and successful people at an obnoxious rate for well over a decade now, and I've put the concepts I've learned into practice—journaling religiously, challenging my old belief system, making vision boards, and practicing gratitude.

I developed the seven-step refuse-to-lose mentality based on all of my research and the wisdom I gained. I follow the steps I outline in this book day in and day out because they work. As a result of the refuse-to-lose process, I'm now at peace with my journey, in love with who I am, pursuing my biggest dreams, and feel more fulfilled than ever before. And I'm still growing every day.

I'm not able to do all of this because I'm exceptional or more capable than other people are. I'm just a normal person who has experienced pain and wanted more. Anyone can do this. *You* can do this. You can rewrite your story and turn your pain into a source of meaning and strength. You just need a process, and that's what the refuse-to-lose mentality will give you. I won't pretend that this process is easy or that it will fix things overnight. It takes a willing attitude and a strong commitment to improve your current state, but if you stick with it, the results will be transformative.

Human beings are the strongest force on the planet. We have built empires, traveled into the unknown, and literally moved mountains. To empower yourself is your birthright as a human. You are infinitely stronger than your past circumstances and adversity, and *you can do this*. Become the hero of your story.

ACKNOWLEDGE YOUR ADVERSITY

The first step to making adversity your advantage is acknowledging your pain.

At a conference I attended, I heard personal development pioneer and teacher Bob Proctor say, "Children are afraid of the dark, and adults are afraid of the light." I found a lot of truth in that statement. We tend to stay in the dark—we hide from ourselves and hide from those things that have caused us the most pain or discomfort. This darkness feels safe, so we believe we're doing what is best for us, without realizing that we're limiting ourselves. We're limiting our progress, growth, and success.

The reason it's so easy to stay in that "safe" dark place

is because our brains are wired for survival. We have a natural instinct to hide from the things that can hurt us, and throughout our lives that instinct grows even stronger due to conditioning and programming. Your brain thinks, *That sexual abuse caused pain, so let's not think about that ever again.* Or, *That death caused pain, so let's not go there anymore.* Every time you do happen to think about it again, you're greeted by pain, reinforcing your brain's instinct to avoid that topic.

If survival was our only goal, this wouldn't matter, but we want to *thrive*, not just survive. If you ever want to move past your adversity and make it your advantage, you must first acknowledge that it exists and is now a part of your journey. If you're in a boat with a hole in it, pretending that the hole doesn't exist won't stop you from sinking; only once you recognize the problem can you begin to take steps to fix it.

MY UNACKNOWLEDGED PAIN

When I was seventeen, a senior at T. W. Andrews High School, a bunch of us students all gathered at Five Points after a Friday-night football game, as was our custom. Five Points was a five-way intersection in High Point with a McDonald's, Family Dollar, and a gas station. I was in the parking lot of the gas station chatting with my friends when gunshots rang out from across the street.

Immediately the atmosphere changed. Commotion, screams, panic, and fear replaced what had been a fun night celebrating another Red Raider victory. I knew somebody had been hit but not who or whether the gunshot was fatal. It was later confirmed on the local news that a stray bullet had killed one of my fellow senior classmates, Jacob Walker. Jacob had been in all my classes. He was the most hilarious guy, with an infectious personality that everyone loved. My school was known for having very talented athletes, and Jacob was no exception. Already a state champion in track and field, Jacob had the kind of speed that would've helped send him to college. I could remember where he was standing that night, about twenty-five yards away from me. One moment, he was cracking jokes with his friends, and the next, he was a story on the eleven o'clock news. He went from being our friend Jacob to, as news reporters said over and over, "the senior T. W. Andrews football player who lost his life Friday night."

Jacob's death was intense and unfamiliar for both the students and faculty of my high school. When such a random, mindless tragedy happens, no one knows what to say or do. I wanted to make sense of it, but I couldn't. I knew that bullet wasn't meant for Jacob. The altercation across the street wasn't planned, and any one of us could've lost our life that night. Jacob's death was traumatic for all of us who knew him but undoubtedly had a unique effect on those of us who were there when it happened. I can't speak for anyone else, but I didn't possess the emotional tools to manage what happened that night. This was the beginning of my close relationship with death.

Then, in April 1998, at the end of my senior year, my best friend at the time, Montre, committed suicide. His death took me completely by surprise.

In July of the previous year, he'd been in a terrible motorcycle accident. Like Jacob, he was a member of the football and track teams, and we didn't know whether he'd ever play again or even make it out alive. Due to third-degree burns from the accident, he had to have extensive skin grafts, which wouldn't allow him to participate in athletic activities. He was worried that he would miss his entire senior season, but he was so determined to get back on the field.

He pulled through and started on the road to recovery. Like most people would in this situation, he gained a new appreciation for his life and the people in it. It was April, nine months after the motorcycle accident and just two months from our high school graduation, when Montre took his life. He had worked hard to become an athlete again, finishing out both the football and track seasons. By the time he committed suicide, it appeared that he'd gotten his life back to normal. It seemed like his life was looking up, and then, just like Jacob, he was gone.

I don't know why Montre chose to take his life. He had never expressed any suicidal thoughts to me. It could have been because of the trauma of a near-death experience, followed by the loss of a close friend. Maybe he was filled with fear, sadness, and anger. Iconic music producer Quincy Jones said this about suicide after his own battle with depression and suicidal thoughts: "I think when people think about taking their own life it's about getting 15 minutes of peace. Just let me get some rest for a while." I think Montre desperately wanted peace.

Again, I don't remember having conversations with anyone about his death. I'm sure people worried about me, but they didn't know how to offer emotional support, guidance, or strategies to cope. I needed therapy, but instead I pretended Montre's suicide hadn't happened. I remember saying out loud to myself, "I'll just act like we both went off to college and won't ever see each other again."

Just as with Jacob's death, my approach to Montre's death was to pretend it hadn't happened. I retreated into that safe, dark place where I thought his death couldn't hurt me.

Six days after Montre died, I signed my National Letter of Intent to play basketball at Wake Forest University, which should have been one of the best feelings of my life, but

I couldn't feel the real joy of that moment. There was no joy. I was broken from the tragedy of my best friend's suicide. Everyone around me was happy and excited for me, for obvious reasons, and they all assumed I felt the same. I didn't, though. I felt deeply sad and, more importantly, alone in my sadness. Pain was accumulating inside of me like a sticky tar. Eventually, I would realize that nobody else was going to fix my pain. Even if they tried, they wouldn't be able to. Others, especially professionals, are here to provide tools and strategies, but we are the ones who must do the work. I had to become my own hero.

Wake Forest was challenging on every front—academically, socially, and even athletically. The school is considered one of the country's finest academic institutions, and with all my ingrained beliefs that I wasn't smart, I always felt as if I was behind my peers. Among A and B students, who appeared to have everything figured out, I was barely surviving with my 2.1 GPA.

On the social front, for the first time, I was introduced to the world of rich, white elite. On my freshman dorm floor, one girl's family owned an island, and another had a black BMW for the winter and a white BMW for the summer. It was a world where young people had no worries outside of which car to drive or where to go for spring break. Most of the other students had lived completely different lives than I had, and I didn't feel as if I belonged. It's hard to feel empowered as an outlier. Wake Forest University didn't have to make adjustments for me, but if I was going to survive, I had to make adjustments for it. Even basketball—the one thing I had always excelled in—had become a challenge because I was now being pushed to perform at a higher level than ever before.

For most of my college career, I felt like the walls were caving in. During my junior year, I fell into a deep depression, experiencing anxiety attacks and suicidal thoughts. I didn't know why I was so hurt and didn't have any tools or steps to deal with the pain. I hadn't yet connected the dots between all my pain points—my adoption, the sexual abuse, the foster kids, seeing Jacob get shot, Montre's suicide, not having my father and mother as a safety net, the struggles of college. I didn't think anyone could understand me and what I'd gone through. I felt deeply alone, and for the first time in my life, I doubted my talent and what I had to offer. In my mind, my significance was tied to my performance in basketball and others' love and approval of me. I'd always desperately wanted acceptance, approval, and love, and the fear of losing those things was intense during my college years.

Sadness and loneliness began to grow within me and gain momentum. Eventually, I began to think of suicide as a solution. Why not? Montre did it. The pain of my life had become unmanageable, and I desperately needed relief. I never followed through on my suicidal thoughts, but they festered deep within my spirit.

Toward the end of my college years, my sadness turned to anger. I hardened to cope. You don't realize you're living in a dysfunctional home until you get out of it. Once I left for college, I started to look around me, and I saw how my teammates' parents demonstrated love and support, coming to take them out to dinner on Friday nights and never missing a game. I compared my peers' childhoods to my own. I looked at their experiences versus mine, and I realized that they had a safe place and people they trusted. They were secure with their closest allies—their parents. I wished I had that. As time went on, I grew increasingly angry. *Of course, I'm struggling,* I thought. *Of course, I'm depressed. How could I not be? Just look at my life.*

Though my college years marked some of the lowest points of my life, they were also the start of my self-discovery. For the first time, I was beginning to acknowledge the adversity and deep, untreated pain of my life. My mom used to always tell me, "What goes on in this house stays in this house." She didn't want me tattling to my grandmother, but I subconsciously interpreted it to mean that you weren't supposed to talk about your adversities or problems or your truth. *Push the pain down, hide it, pretend it doesn't exist, try to outrun it, and hope it doesn't catch up.* I can tell you from personal experience that those strategies don't work. If you don't acknowledge your pain, it will bubble to the surface eventually.

Though I could broadly identify my traumas at this point in my life, I still hadn't fully acknowledged them. An important part of acknowledging your adversity is understanding how your pain has influenced you, and I couldn't do that. I was still stuck in a victim mentality. I knew that Jacob's and Montre's deaths, my absent father, and my dysfunctional childhood home were major pain points for me, but I didn't understand how those traumas had contributed to my view of myself and the world around me. I knew there was a hole in the boat, but I had no idea where the hole was or how it was affecting the entire vessel.

CONTINUAL SELF-DISCOVERY

The way we see ourselves—our self-image and our self-identity—is everything. And our adversity, our pain, our experiences, and our circumstances all have roles in creating that self-image. In Chapter 3, "Rewrite Your Story," I'll talk more about rewriting your story and creating a new self-image for yourself. First, it's important to focus on the current story you're telling yourself.

The key to determining your self-identity is self-discovery, and self-discovery is all about awareness. It's about understanding more and understanding better. The core of self-discovery is asking and answering questions: *Who am I? What am I here to do? What is this experience supposed to teach me? What things are limiting me? What are my inherent beliefs? What paradigms are preventing me from moving forward? Who do I spend my time with? How do these people affect me? What do I need to shift to reach my goals?* By discovering the answers to such questions, you can begin to align your mind, body, and spirit and become the best, most fulfilled version of yourself.

I believe that we should be in a constant state of self-discovery. We are changing shape and form every second of every day. The process of developing is nonstop, even in our sleep. You may know exactly who you are one day, but who you are is going to change, so self-discovery must continue. We are moving, creative beings. Energy flows and moves through us all the time, and new ideas come to us every second. You will never reach a point in your journey where you can say, "Okay, I'm done. I have no more growing to do." The day you stop growing is the day you die.

At one point in time, I assumed I would always be a basketball coach. But our old ways may not always work for us. That's why continual self-discovery is so important. I loved being a basketball coach, but I grew into a different person. After fourteen years, I realized that I was being too loyal to my old way of living, and I resigned. It was time for me to stop being Adell Harris, the basketball coach, and focus on being Adell Harris, the inspirational speaker, author, and personal development coach who experienced deep pain but found a way to make it work to her advantage. As I more fully acknowledged painful points of my story, I experienced healing and growth, and I am now able to teach other people how to make their experiences work for them. That has become my new purpose.

Life is always challenging us to make these shifts. Maybe you want to be a great mother or father. But someday, your kids will grow up and leave the house, and your identity will have to shift. Perhaps you lose someone close to you or receive a cancer diagnosis; your world will change, and so you will be required to change, too. When faced with life changes, you have to shift your purpose, beliefs, and identity, asking yourself, "How am I going to live my life now?" Many times, pain can lead us to a greater purpose but only when we allow it. For example, a loved one's cancer diagnosis could inspire you to organize a fundraiser for research.

Every day, you should wake up and take inventory of your happiness, goals, and purpose. Ask yourself, "Who am I? Is my spirit aligned with my thoughts and my actions?" Without continual self-discovery, you are limiting yourself to your old ways, closing the door on any new opportunities.

EMPOWERING QUESTIONS

Conversation with yourself is vitally important for continual self-discovery, which necessarily involves an acknowledgment of your pain. In this conversation, you can choose whether to ask yourself limiting questions or empowering questions.

Limiting questions tend to be rhetorical. They won't allow for good answers, and they aren't designed to help you grow and move forward. They are often blaming or pitying questions that put you into a victim mindset. *Why me? Why am I the one who has to deal with this? How is this fair? Why don't I get treated like everyone else? Why didn't my dad love me? How could my boyfriend do that to me? Why did so-and-so do x, y, or z?*

You can't control anyone's actions but your own, and nobody has the power to make you feel better except you. Thus, the process of healing your pain must be internal to external, not external to internal. Limiting questions are outside-in, meaning that when you ask limiting questions, you are attempting to find external answers to internal problems. Personal development guru Tony Robbins has said that if you don't like your answers, ask different questions. Limiting questions won't give you the answers you need, so ask empowering questions instead. Empowering questions are inside-out. By asking empowering, self-discovery questions, you can work on finding your internal answers, which will reflect in your external life as well.

Questions are empowering when they can motivate you to take action—to address the problem and fix it. The power is knowing: *I am in control of the questions I ask, which makes me in control of the story I write. I own this. I'm the person in this story that matters most.*

To acknowledge your pain, ask yourself these two empowering questions:

- Where is my pain, challenge, or adversity?
- What is the story I'm telling myself?

These questions are empowering because they reveal your starting point. They give you clarity on where you are right now.

Where is your pain, challenge, or adversity? Dig deep with this question. Peel back the layers of your pain or challenge. After determining where the pain is, ask yourself, "What is underneath that pain?" In my case, I could point to my relationship with my mother and my childhood as sources of pain. But why were those experiences painful? As I explored more, I realized that at the root of my pain was rejection and abandonment. My biological parents didn't want me. My mom didn't express her love for me in the way I thought a mother should. My dad wasn't there for me either. Over fifty foster children had come in and out of my life, never to be seen again. In a way, even Jacob and Montre had left me. I internalized all of those experiences, and it made me extremely sensitive to abandonment and rejection. That sensitivity controlled all my interpersonal relationships.

Once I understood the basis of my pain, I understood myself better. I understood why it stung so much when people told me or made me feel like I wasn't good enough, and I understood why it hurt so much when people that I loved left my life. That was the first step to learning how to handle rejection better. Since I recognize that rejection and abandonment are my triggers, I can quickly identify limiting thoughts when they arise and respond differently.

You can do this process backwards too. Instead of starting with an experience you know was painful for you, start with something you currently struggle with. For example, I've struggled with developing a healthy definition of sex and its relationship with love. By asking myself, "What contributes to my unhealthy view of sex? What is the pain behind this?" I've just recently come to realize that my views on sex, sexual language, and sexual behavior were driven by shame, guilt, fear, and embarrassment.

My mother worked at the health department, and she talked to me and many others about the dangers of sexually transmitted diseases and was an advocate for safe sex, but she didn't teach me how love and sex were related. My home was drowning in both sexual language and sexual behavior but lacking in love. To me, marriage didn't mean love, and neither did sex. Sex was an action used by hurt people who were in search of love and significance. Without me knowing it, my paradigm caused me to judge and look down on people that treated sex according to my childhood definition of it.

It wasn't until much later in life that I realized how beautiful sex was. It might very well be God's greatest gift to us. Sexual energy is a real thing, and we all have an innate desire to express ourselves through sexual thoughts, language, and actions. I now believe sex is not an explicit, carnal act but intimacy at its most authentic level and something that should be reserved for someone you love. For a lot of us, it takes time to figure this out.

My unhealthy view of sex had stopped me from evolving, but by working backward to identify the pain affecting me in this area, I've been able to move forward with confidence to the next steps of the refuse-to-lose process and have begun to rewrite my limiting beliefs.

After determining where your pain is, turn your attention to the story you're telling yourself about your pain. Often the stories we tell ourselves are based on lies. We adopt those lies as our language, with our thoughts and feelings reinforcing the lies until we accept them as truth. Our behavior follows our thoughts and feelings, and so the lies manifest into action in our physical world.

You can change this story and choose to stop believing the lies, but first you have to identify the story you're telling yourself. Maybe the story is "I will never attract a good man because good men simply don't exist" or "I'm black, so I'm never going to get that promotion" or "It's impossible for me to lose weight, as obesity runs in my family."

We all create stories to rationalize our behaviors. Stories have power. If the story you tell yourself is limiting, then you're giving power to external forces instead of internal ones. You can only ever rise to your self-image—that is, you can only achieve what you *believe* is possible for you to achieve. Tell yourself an empowering story, and you will be able to achieve so much more.

SOURCES OF PAIN

All of us have different sources of pain in our lives. Maybe you've had a miscarriage. Perhaps you've gone through a divorce or had your heart broken. Maybe something or someone made you feel less than you are. Maybe you want to go back to school, but you don't have the courage to pursue your dream. Perhaps your parents did their best but were not attentive. Maybe you feel isolated or stuck. Maybe you have a pretty good life but feel like something is missing. You can have a fake-perfect Instagram and Facebook life and still suffer from pain.

We all have unspoken needs and challenges. Luckily, it's never too late to learn the skills needed to make adversity your advantage, and you've already begun down that path by picking up this book.

When you're trying to determine the origins of your pain, it can be helpful to focus on three main sources of pain: environment, addiction, and identity.

ENVIRONMENT

The biggest source of pain is your environment, both past and present.

Your environment is the space you operate in every day— the things you see, feel, and hear day in and day out. Your environment affects who you are more than anything else, and it is often why you're not getting the results you want in life, why you feel discomfort and pain, and why you feel like your walls are closing in.

Environment controls your behavior, your actions, and who you become. If you're confused about who you are and where your pain is, you should check your past and present environment. In my time on college campuses, I've witnessed a lot of situations surrounding young men's mistreatment of women. I believe our challenge as leaders is to learn more about the environment these young men grew up in. If they were raised in environments where women commonly suffered from domestic violence, verbal abuse, or sexual abuse, then of course they're more likely to perpetuate such actions, because our environment is what creates our belief systems, which are the foundation of our identity—who we are.

People make up a huge component of your environment and are a frequent source of pain because they will put their limitations on you. Some people will tear you down and tell you that you can't do something. The words they use will hurt: "You're not going to be good at this." "That's a dumb idea." "You're not smart like so-and-so." "You're not pretty like so-and-so."

I can only speak to the specific messages I have received

as a black woman. All my life, people and society put me in a box, attempting to decide my future before I got a chance to create it on my own. What are the specific messages you have received? Have you internalized others' preconceived limitations of you, accepting them as part of your story? These insecurities create internal conflict and affect the way you view the world, your potential, and your role in society. Don't let others determine your fate. As motivational speaker Les Brown said, "Your opinion of me doesn't have to become my reality."

A big part of environment we don't talk about enough is money. When I was growing up, we never had conversations about money. It always felt like a big secret. I knew nothing about our money situation, other than us not having enough of it. Economic pressure is a significant source of pain, and we *should* talk about it. It plays a major role in our lives. It's stressful to not have enough money to provide for basic necessities like food and shelter. Even if you have enough money for the necessities, you may not have enough to pursue your dreams and become all you want to be.

Economic pressure can affect anyone. Many times, people who grew up poor will adopt a mindset of lack that continues into adulthood, even if they are making a comfortable income. You can be a millionaire and still feel as if you don't have "enough." The suicide rate for white men is rising, and I think one contributor is economic pressure. I believe they feel pressure to try to live up to the economic standards that society has built for them, and when they fail, they can't handle it.

Perhaps you are dealing with a constant economic pressure, or maybe you've been thrust into financial uncertainty due to a life event, like the loss of your job.

Life events can come at us unexpectedly, triggering old belief systems and causing a great deal of pain. At any moment, you can get the call that your mom or dad died, that someone you love more than anything is no longer here. Traumatic events catch us off guard, and we're left to grieve over the loss of a loved one or the end of a marriage or whatever it may be. These course-altering events are part of life, and this book will give you tools to move forward through them in a process of growth and personal development.

When faced with unexpected life events and the pressures of everyday life, we often feel overwhelmed and anxious. We feel pressure to live up to the expectations we have for ourselves, as well as the expectations of our peers, our family, and society. We're trying to be enough for everybody. You get your degree, walk across the stage to accept your diploma, and then you're an "adult" in the real world. Now you're overwhelmed and wondering,

Okay, how do I pay my bills? How do I get this job? If you are further along in life, you can feel overwhelmed for all kinds of other reasons. The pressure can be constant if you let it be, and the weight of that pressure can be a source of pain for you.

ADDICTION

Addiction can also be a major source of pain, whether it be addiction to alcohol, drugs, tobacco (which killed my grandmother and so many others), food, gambling, or even sex. Nearly everyone has dealt with an addiction issue, either firsthand or secondhand through a friend or family member. Addiction doesn't care about your skin color or where you were raised or how much money you have. It affects people universally.

Though I've struggled with alcohol, I've been fortunate to not be exposed to too much drug addiction. Drugs have always been a major issue in our country, though, and things are no different today. Crystal meth and opioids are affecting young people at a high rate, and these addictions kill people.

Food addiction is also a serious issue and can lead to obesity and diabetes. My mom died at sixty-two as a diabetic because she could not control or own that part of her life. Even on her deathbed she surrendered to her food addiction. She refused to follow the diet plan her doctors gave her to extend her life, and she died sooner than she had to.

Many addictions stem from some underlying pain. Children who suffer sexual abuse and those who are exposed to sex too early or in a negative way often struggle with sex addiction later in life due to their untreated trauma. Sex can become a compulsion for them, and some become abusers themselves.

Kirk Franklin, a gospel singer and music producer whom I admire, admitted to having an addiction to pornography, saying, "I saw my first pornographic magazine at the age of eight or nine, and from that point I was addicted." By admitting his addiction, he was able to more fully acknowledge the trauma he had experienced as a child and how it continued to affect him as an adult. Only then was he able to begin the healing process.

Addiction is a double-edged sword. Many times, deep-seated pain will manifest as an addiction, and then the addiction will create new hurts, new adversities. A lot of people are hospitalized each year due to addiction, and addiction has a ripple effect on those around the addict. Many of the foster kids I grew up with had parents who were addicted to alcohol or drugs. Their parents' addiction affected them, putting them at greater risk for similar toxic behaviors. Everything we do affects others, particularly when we become adults and raise children or are in any position of authority, responsible for leading others.

IDENTITY

The world is changing. Attitudes about race, gender, and sexual identity are shifting, and in twenty-five years I firmly believe society will be more accepting as a whole. But discrimination still happens and will continue to happen, and it is a significant source of adversity, because we all want to feel like we belong and are important.

The desire to be accepted and belong can force us to hide who we are. I fully embrace who I am now, but that wasn't always the case. It's been difficult for me to be unapologetically me and to love all of myself in every environment. My black friends would say I acted too white, while to white America, being too black was a threat. I would adjust my behavior, trying to fit into whatever box a particular situation seemed to require of me. But not accepting who you truly are, not loving yourself completely, causes pain. I should have been proud of who I was. If others don't give us permission to be ourselves, we *must* have the courage to do it for ourselves. There is no greater example of celebrating who you are than James Brown's song "Say It Loud—I'm Black and I'm Proud."

A couple of years ago, while I was in deep study of successful black businesswomen, I met a woman named Mellody Hobson. Mellody is a brilliant woman who is currently the president of Ariel Investments and soon to be vice chair of Starbucks. In an interview with *Fortune* magazine, Mellody shared a story that changed my life:

> At John Johnson's [founder of *Ebony* and *Jet* magazines] funeral Tom Joyner got up to give his eulogy and he said "John Johnson was unapologetically black" and when I heard it, I froze. All I could think about was that I had been apologizing for who I am. I had been apologizing for being a woman. I had been apologizing for being black and today it stops. I had been tip toeing around these things but today that ends.[2]

I am now an unapologetically proud gay black woman. I understand that all the many layers of my personality and spirit work together to enhance those facts. If I don't love all of me, then I am limiting the full expression of who I am and who I can become. It is my duty to live the most elevated and empowered life that I can while I'm on this earth.

Religion can be a major source of identity conflict, especially if you are gay, black, and from the South like me. One of the issues with religion is that what people believe

---

2 "Mellody Hobson Discusses Discrimination at MPW Next Gen," interview by Leigh Gallagher, *Fortune Magazine*, December 15, 2014, video, 21:46, https://youtu.be/sVia3ZHcsjI.

in is man's interpretation of something far greater. People will thus use their religion as an excuse to validate their personal disapproval of who you are. Throughout slavery and the civil rights movement, white America would use God to justify their racist conduct, claiming, "*God* doesn't want whites and blacks together." A white man could be the mayor, the pastor, and the grand wizard, all in the name of Jesus. It's funny to think about, but this is one example of how man has abused religion to support inequality and racism for years.

Because of how people have used religion to discriminate, many have given up on religion. On *The Dick Cavett Show* in 1968, James Baldwin said he stopped believing in the Christian church when he realized there were different churches for black people and white people. If religion was truly about love, he could see no reason for separate churches:

> I don't know if white Christians hate Negroes or not; I know that we have a Christian church which is white and a Christian church which is black. I know as Malcolm X once put it, "The most segregated hour in American life is high noon on Sunday. That says a great deal to me about a Christian nation." It means that I can't afford to trust most white Christians and certainly cannot trust the Christian church.

Personally, I work to accept everyone without judgment.

I believe that God knows me better than I know myself, and despite my mistakes, sexual orientation, or skin color, his love for me is unwavering.

If you try to hide part of who you are, you will create internal conflict. I speak from personal experience: this internal battle will stand in the way of your personal growth and development. Many people have been driven to suicide because they were not able to fully express themselves. I want to encourage you: be true to yourself and stay away from people who make you feel bad for being who you are.

With all three of these categories, it's important to ask those empowering questions: *Where is my pain, challenge, or adversity? What is the story I'm telling myself?* Then you can move on to the next steps of the process: accepting the pain and working to rewrite your story and create a new self-image.

ROADBLOCKS TO ACKNOWLEDGING YOUR PAIN

Many of us know that we carry pain, but we never concretely identify and face that pain. We know our challenges. We know our unspoken wounds. We know where we're insecure, how we feel when we're rejected, and when we have self-doubt. We know what that broken heart did to us. We know that our dad not being there when we were growing up is affecting us to this day.

We know these things, but we're conditioned to not say anything—to ignore the pain, put on a happy face, and act like it didn't happen, like it's not our truth. We go out into the world and show everyone what we think they want to see. The world doesn't give us permission to identify and face our pain, but we must impose our will and own our outcome for our personal survival. It's not enough to know what trauma is hiding in the dark recesses of your mind. If you let your pain stay in the dark, it will never go away; it will always be there, a dark shadow in your life. Instead, I encourage you to flip on the light and really see your pain. There is no true strength here without true vulnerability.

After you go through this seven-step process, your pain will still be there, but it will have a new shape and form, and it will affect you in a different way. You will have transformed it from something negative and horrible into something beautiful that you can use as a tool to be your best self. Instead of your pain having power over you, you will realize that *you* are the power that happens to have the pain.

Flipping on the light is the first step, but we're frequently held back by fear, anger, or guilt and shame.

FEAR

You might be afraid of what other people will say, afraid to go against your inherited belief systems and paradigms, or, on the most basic level, afraid to feel your pain.

Your brain wants to keep you safe. Its primary job is to keep you alive, and to your brain, pain is a bright-red flag saying, *Stop! Don't go here!* Your brain will compensate for your deficiencies in order to avoid pain. If your right hip hurts, then your left hip, left leg, back, or shoulders will shift in order to ease the pain. The same thing happens in your life. Your brain creates stories to rationalize the way you behave and act. But ultimately, it's your responsibility to know there's some damn pain in your right hip, and you need to do something about it.

Confronting fear and adversity can feel overwhelming. Nobody wants to say, "I was sexually abused." I think back to the *Oprah Winfrey Show* episode where a studio full of sexually abused men shared their story, including actor, writer, and producer Tyler Perry. Grown men wept upon sharing their experiences around childhood sexual abuse because they'd never been able to tell anybody before. At times in my life, I was afraid that I wouldn't be able to handle everything. I felt as if I'd fall apart or explode. I felt like I was barely hanging on and couldn't take any more. Life was hard enough on its own, and I felt that I'd rather deal with what is as opposed to dealing with the unknown. How could I possibly go back and address all my untreated traumas? I didn't have the time, energy, or willpower.

Your brain wants you to keep doing what you've always been doing, because that's familiar and "safe." But life will force you to deal with who you are eventually. For my sake, I couldn't afford *not* to address my pain. I finally reached the point where it was time. I was tired of carrying my pain, and I didn't care whether I exploded or what that explosion might look like. I needed to put myself first, and I did.

If you're feeling overwhelmed and unable to address your pain, I want you to think about all the times in your past when you dealt with adversity. You're still here, aren't you? You survived. You've already demonstrated strength in difficult situations. *You can do this.* You are capable of getting to the other side of whatever hurdle is currently in front of you.

We can gain strength from our history. I do this often. Oftentimes I need to remind myself that I got out of my dysfunctional childhood house and made a better life for myself. I don't have a father, mother, or grandmother to call, but I am out here in the world, contributing in a positive way, serving people to the best of my ability, and living my dreams. Sometimes we need to remind ourselves how incredible we really are, because we *are* incredible. We so easily lose sight of that fact.

ANGER

Fear isn't all that gets in the way on our road to acknowledging pain; we can also be held back by anger. This is a secondary emotion that is rooted in sadness. We don't get permission to simply be sad, so we act out our sadness in anger. Sadness makes us feel weak, and anger makes us feel in control. I witnessed this firsthand with the foster kids I grew up with. Their sadness had turned into anger, and this anger became a physical energy that lived in my home. They would get angry and throw things, slam doors, fight each other, and cry aggressively out of rage. Underneath it all, they were hurting. I've experienced those outbursts of anger and violent tears from sadness myself. Unlocking the sadness behind your anger is key.

Anger can be a gift—a powerful energy source. It can help you achieve your goals and fulfill your purpose. Hip-hop music is a great example of the power of anger in action. I'm a huge fan of hip-hop. I believe it's the most ambitious art form created to date. These artists have taken their anger and the anger of their communities and created an entire musical genre. They've used their gifts and talents to give a voice to the deep anger and sadness in their communities, and in doing so, they've helped others feel less alone. Today, hip-hop dominates pop culture and is the most influential sound of the last two decades.

The civil rights movement is another example of the power of anger filtered into action. Martin Luther King Jr., Ralph Abernathy, Rosa Parks, James Baldwin, and other activists fought for a better life for African Americans. There's no way those people weren't at times angry, but they didn't lash out or let their anger control them. Instead, they used that energy to start a movement. They flipped anger on its head and used it in the service of love. They used it to speak light to the dark and make the world a better, more-just place. They used their talents to speak words of empowerment and to inspire confidence. They challenged others to not lose their cool but to use their minds while organizing nonviolent protests around the country to clearly communicate their demand for equality. Anger turned into a movement, a force so strong that we must forever refer to it when discussing our country's history.

I've spent time with veterans, and many of them struggle with anger. They lived in stressful, dangerous environments, constantly on edge, waiting for unseen enemies to attack. Some of them watched their friends die or were injured themselves. Then, when they come home, they're still living with those physical, emotional, and psychological wounds. In some ways, they've had the best training in the world to ensure that they don't deal with adversity. They must be able to execute orders in high-stress situations, and they can't let emotions get in the way. In addition, veterans tend to be deeply patriotic, with a strong desire to protect others. In the service, that warrior mentality serves them well, but at home, the world doesn't work that way. Many veterans thus feel like outcasts when they return home, unable to determine how they fit into this different world. All of this leads to deep loneliness and sorrow, and as is so common in the world, that deep pain manifests as anger. This anger can hold them back and prevent them from acknowledging the hurt inside.

Anger, like pain, is authentic. It's raw. It inspires people. When you can transform your anger into something of value, I believe you can change the world. If not wisely channeled, though, anger can lock you in and shut you off from others.

Eventually, our anger can transform into depression, which kills. I mean it when I say that adversity kills. I know because I've been there. I have wanted to harm myself. I have also felt angry enough that if someone had come at me in the wrong way at the wrong time, I think I could have seriously hurt them.

What about you? Are you angry? Why? What pain is

behind your anger? And how are you using your anger? Is your anger a shield to keep everyone and everything at a distance, or is your anger a tool, an energy driving you forward?

GUILT AND SHAME

Sometimes, when we've gone through something but don't know how to handle it, we hurt people. We hurt others and we hurt ourselves. We lash out in ways that we're not proud of, continuing a cycle of guilt and shame. Dr. George Pratt, a California neuropsychologist, has said, "Guilt seeks punishment subconsciously." We self-sabotage. We don't think we deserve love, so even when we find love, we sabotage it. Because of this lack of self-worth, we can become depressed and think that people can never understand us, so we shut them out.

I've gone through that self-sabotaging process many times. I'll think, *Nobody understands me, and even if I try to explain it to them, they still won't get it.* It's easier to keep my feelings to myself, to not trust people, and to not be open and vulnerable. But we weren't designed to be alone. Human beings need each other for almost everything. Loneliness does not lead to a life of abundance, empowerment, joy, and freedom.

Even if you don't like how you handled a situation in

the past, don't be too critical of yourself. There are no perfect people. You did the best you could with the knowledge and resources you had at the time. You were acting according to who you were and where you were in your journey at that time. As the late great Dr. Maya Angelou would say, if you had known better, you would have done better. We can be so hard on ourselves that we don't give ourselves permission to move forward. Forgive yourself for past mistakes and focus on how you can do things differently this time. Today is a new beginning.

I handled my adversity by drinking a lot. Self-medicating is a thing. I'm not proud of that. I feel deeply embarrassed and terrible about that decision. I drove drunk many nights and could have killed somebody. But I also know that I don't have to be perfect, and accepting my past mistakes without judgment is part of accepting and acknowledging the fullness of my story.

We need to accept ourselves, and we need to keep moving forward. You've made mistakes in the past, and you will make more in the future. You have to be okay with the fact that a horrible decision you made may have impacted someone else's life in a terrible way, and sometimes you have to be okay with other people not forgiving you. Instead, you have to forgive yourself and then move on. Don't stay stuck in that place where other people want you to stay. Ex-convicts have to learn this like no one else. They go through their rehabilitation but are often still viewed as criminals. Like they must learn to do, you should work to tune out the voices of others when it comes to you and your mistakes. Otherwise, you will be trapped in a mental prison. Rather than hiding, I believe that only honesty and forgiveness can allow us to move past the guilt and shame.

WAYS TO ACKNOWLEDGE YOUR PAIN

The best way to acknowledge your pain is to work on self-awareness, which I've already touched on briefly. It amazes me how many of us walk through life never getting to know ourselves. We don't ask empowering questions, and so we don't acknowledge our pain. Remember the two core empowering questions you must answer: *Where is my pain, challenge, or adversity?* and *What's the story I'm telling myself?*

You must also be aware and honest about your behaviors. The world will give you clues that your behavior is off. You have to learn to admit when you've acted wrongly. I've had to admit that the way I treated my mother was wrong. I've had to admit that my behavior around alcohol was toxic. I'm open and willing to admit when my behavior is out of line and negative. I tell myself, "Adell, stop defending your bad behavior." That is the first step to adopting healthier habits. Ownership and accountability are vital.

Your behavior comes from your thoughts and feelings, which are internal. Everything you demonstrate to the outside world reflects who you are inside. If you cuss, scream, and shout, it's because of what is going on inside. If you drink all the time, if you judge people who are different from you, if you overeat or have a poor self-image, it's because of what's happening internally. Explore those thoughts and feelings.

I suggest performing self-audits regularly. At least four times a year, ask yourself, *Who am I? What am I supposed to learn from my journey at this moment? Are the people around me helping me or hurting me? Is my environment conducive to nurturing my goals and dreams? Who do I want to be?*

I highly recommend journaling your self-audit. Sitting down and putting pen to paper forces you to think more deeply about these questions and your answers. Plus, it gives you a documented history of your growth. You can return to previous entries and see clearly how you've progressed.

As I will discuss further in Chapter 3, "Rewrite Your Story," the vision you have of yourself will manifest externally. If I *know* that I'm a strong, smart, confident black gay woman, it's only a matter of time before I demonstrate that externally. We rise to the level of our self-image. By understanding and asking yourself these empowering questions, you can live the life you want.

ACKNOWLEDGE IT

In our society, we rarely communicate the harsh reality of things. We want to sweep everything under the rug and ignore it. We want to arrive at a positive place without communicating our truth. Harsh realities must be told, though. Otherwise the issues linger. They become sores, which become cancers that can kill us. Addressing the harsh reality is the first step toward progression and growth. I believe that our country is suffering because of an unwillingness to openly communicate its flaws. Ego is the enemy of internal growth.

Vernon Howard said, "You cannot escape a prison when you don't know you're in one." Pain can certainly be a prison, and if you don't acknowledge the sources of your pain, you have no chance of escaping.

ACCEPT YOUR ADVERSITY

It's not enough to just acknowledge your pain; you must *accept* it. The opposite of *accept* is *reject*, so if you are not accepting your pain, you must be rejecting it. Your pain is part of who you are, so by rejecting your pain, you are rejecting *yourself*.

All your hurt and trauma, as painful as it is, made you into the person you are today. As counterintuitive as it may seem, *your pain is a good thing*, because it has forced you to access strength you didn't know you had. Your pain has not broken you; it has forged you into the beautiful, powerful individual you are today. For you to make adversity your advantage, you have to believe that your pain produced a power that is in your best interest.

I own the fact that I was sexually abused and that I grew up in a verbally abusive home. I own the fact that I lost loved ones. I own the fact that I often drank myself to sleep. I own it. It's mine. It's my journey, my story, and it's the only one I have.

Your pain is part of you, and you must love yourself completely, pain included. Practicing complete self-love and acceptance allows you to give that to others as well. You will never be able to fully accept others if you can't fully accept yourself. I know I wasn't able to completely accept my mother until I could accept myself.

When you adopt pure love for your journey, your pain, and yourself, you empower yourself to go forward and do whatever you want to do with your life.

MY WAKE-UP CALL

When I was twenty-four, on December 3, 2004, I got a call from my mother telling me that my maternal grandmother had stage IV lung cancer. I remember not really knowing what "stage IV" meant and naively asking when chemo would start. Chemo was all I knew about cancer. My mom explained that my grandmother was too sick to get chemo and that there was nothing the doctors could do for her. I'd seen her at Thanksgiving, and she'd been lively, dancing to jazz music in the living room with my brother. Two months after the diagnosis, on February 13, she was gone.

For all my life, I'd always felt that nobody really loved me unless I could provide something for them, and usually that something had to do with the sport of basketball. They loved my abilities, not me. So Adell Harris, the basketball player, was loved; Adell Harris, the person, was not. My grandmother, on the other hand, loved me unconditionally. She loved me enough for ten thousand people, and I loved her back fiercely.

I took her death very hard and did not handle it in a healthy way. I angrily rejected a life without my grandmother in it. There was no accepting, embracing, or loving anything about it. Everything—my issues around being adopted and feeling the need to go above and beyond to be accepted by people, the years of verbal abuse at home, the sexual abuse and dysfunction, and not dealing with the deaths of my two high school friends—all of it came to a head, and my walls finally came crashing down.

I began drinking more heavily and regularly, from two days a week, to three, to four. Before long, I was getting drunk five days a week. Internally, my life was falling apart, but externally I managed to put on a great disguise. I was an assistant coach at the University of North Carolina (UNC) Asheville, and I hid behind basketball.

Underneath, all my unspoken wounds were still there, and eventually they were bound to come to the surface.

I finally hit rock bottom in February 2009 when I received a DUI. I was caught driving the wrong way down a one-way street with a blood alcohol concentration almost three times the legal limit. My driver's license was suspended, and I attended mandatory DUI classes. My internal battles had spilled over into my external life. The unresolved pain from my past was a distraction and could've been the end of my professional success up to that point.

My DUI was a wake-up call. I could see that it was a direct consequence of not dealing with my adversities, so I made a decision—drew a line in the sand. *I'm better than this,* I decided. *All these things I'm doing—all these toxic behaviors and self-medicating—are not working for me. I'm going to face my pain head on, and I'm going to own my outcome.*

I had already acknowledged my pain before this point, but I hadn't been able to *accept* it. I'd been stuck in a victim mentality. I was determined to change that.

YOUR PAIN DOES NOT DEFINE YOU

Throughout our lives, we tend to define ourselves according to external events. We lose a loved one or suffer abuse or have our hearts broken, and we define ourselves by that pain. For a long time, I framed my sexual abuse in terms of "me." *I* was sexually abused—that's who I was. But I eventually realized that my sexual abuse is *not* me. The sexual abuse is an event that occurred to my physical body, but my identity comes from inside. Our power comes from inside.

Our thoughts, our imagination, our emotions, our will, our self-awareness—all are aspects of our internal world. They're our unique human gifts, and if we master and hone them every day, these gifts become tools that allow us to create the life we want to live. I truly believe that all the answers you need lie within you.

While your pain is *part* of your experience, it is not who you are, and it doesn't have to define who you'll become. It is not the whole of your being. We're not *one* circumstance. We're not *one* event. We are not *one* day, *one* situation, or *one* relationship with one person.

Just as you need to accept your pain, you also need to accept your potential. I remind myself daily that I am God's greatest form of creation. He has created me to have infinite potential, to have infinite possibilities, and to accomplish anything. When I am faced with setbacks and struggles, I tell myself, "I can't be *this* small. I can't

be *this one thing*. My existence has to be more than that."
I believe my good friend Montre would still be here if he
would've asked himself these questions.

Whatever your personal beliefs are, part of accepting your
pain is also accepting that *you are greater than your pain*.

THE UNFAIRNESS OF PAIN

It's easy to get stuck in thinking that your pain is unfair
and shouldn't have happened to you. You may look at
other people and think, *Why did these things happen to
me? None of these people have to deal with my pain. It isn't
fair that I have to.* And you know what? You're right—to
an extent. Much of pain *is* unfair. Lots of things in my
life have been unfair, but I can't—and you can't—live life
on "unfair." We have to put an expiration date on that
mindset, or we will never move forward.

If you're stuck in unfair, you're probably going to fall into
the role of victim or villain. You can live your whole life
in those roles if you want, but if you do, nothing will ever
change. Remember: nobody's coming to save you. You
must be your own hero.

To determine whether you're playing the victim or villain, look for BCD language: blaming, complaining, and
defending. Ask yourself, "Am I blaming? Am I complain-

ing? Am I defending myself or my bad behaviors?" If so, you're probably acting out the role of victim or villain.

You aren't doing yourself any favors by getting stuck in an unfairness mindset. In an interview with Charlie Rose in 1995, around the peak of the Chicago Bulls dynasty with Michael Jordan, head coach Phil Jackson said, "Adversity and not handling difficult situations correctly can be a distraction. A lot of individuals are good enough to win, but they get distracted along the way."

You are good enough to win—but you can't let yourself get distracted by adversity along the way. If you learn to handle difficult situations correctly and turn your adversity into your advantage, your potential will be unlimited.

VICTIM, VILLAIN, HERO

In our stories, we're either the victim, the villain, or the hero. This is the three-part drama triangle taught in drama school, and it represents all the personalities of your ego. You can't fully eliminate the victim or villain aspects of your ego, but you can choose to play the role of hero and give more weight to that part of your personality.

When it comes to incorrect ways to handle adversity, victim and villain mindsets are top of the list. These mindsets are the opposite of acceptance; they are manifestations of us rejecting our pain. When you play victim or villain, you are allowing your pain to have power over you when it should be the other way around.

VICTIM

The victim is a weak person wanting someone to come and save them. When you're the victim, you judge people for not saving you. You hold them to an impossible standard, making it *their* responsibility to improve *your* life. It is your journey, your life, and no one else can step in and be the hero for you.

If you experience something traumatic, the world will give you permission to be a victim—but not for long. No matter how terrible your adversity, the world quickly stops caring. Just think about the victims of a mass shooting or a destructive natural disaster. We talk about it for a few days, a few months tops, and then nobody talks about how somebody lost a mother, a son, a best friend. It's up to those people to go on and live their lives.

When things catch you off guard, you're allowed to be a victim temporarily. Sometimes you will need help and support, and others will help prop you up for a while. But eventually they're going to stop. They have their own lives to live and can't be responsible for championing you every day. At a certain point it will be *your* full-time job to come out of that victim stage. You can't pitch a tent in victimhood and camp out there. If you do, you will fall into a toxic victim mentality, where you become a blaming, complaining, defending individual. Life doesn't stop for anyone. Life asks that you continue to grow, learn, and become a new version of yourself after the event or pain has occurred.

I've been the victim, thinking, *Why did my mom treat me that way? Why didn't my dad do this?* I waited for my mom or my dad or *someone* to come save me. I was waiting and waiting, and after a while I realized, *They're not coming. Nobody's coming to save you. You have to save yourself.*

A key aspect of victim mentality is an overwhelming focus on problems and pain instead of on solutions and ways to move forward. When you identify as a victim, your pain and sadness turn into self-pity, which then turns into complaining and blaming people all the time. You feel sorry for yourself and look for someone to come rescue you. That behavior is toxic and dangerous, and it will certainly prevent you from making adversity your advantage. You are essentially giving up ownership of your life, convincing yourself that you are not strong enough, resilient enough, and powerful enough to achieve your dreams.

The four main characteristics of victim behavior are

hopelessness, self-destructive behavior, lack of belief in oneself, and fear of change.

Hopelessness is the most dangerous aspect of victimhood. The last thing you want to be is hopeless. That is where people commit suicide and hurt or even kill others. When you have no hope for a better future, when you can see no way through your adversity, you can make reckless, harmful decisions.

I've been in this position before. I know what it feels like to think things will never get better, to feel as if I'm trapped in a bottomless pit with no light, no hope of escape, and no idea what I'm supposed to do next. Hopelessness is where depression lives, and it leads to self-destructive behaviors such as anorexia, overeating, sexual promiscuity, alcoholism, drug addiction, and suicidal ideation. It leads to things that kill you.

Oftentimes, though, people suffering from the victim mentality aren't self-destructive. They live basic, normal lives, and on the surface, it may not seem as if anything is wrong. Things are "good enough." They've accepted their lot in life and have given up on achieving more because they don't believe that they *deserve* better. They're stuck, held back by limiting circumstances or limiting belief systems.

Not believing in yourself and in your greatness is a poor

way to exist. You've been put here with infinite potential, in a world full of abundance, to accept who you are and to do great things without limitations or lack. There are trillions of dollars and countless opportunities in this world. There's no reason why you should adopt a belief of poverty, or of lack, or of "I'm not good enough."

You may fear change. You may want things to remain the same because you are comfortable where you are. What new opportunities are going to present themselves? Will you be willing to take the risk and jump? When you're afraid of the change that tomorrow might bring, you demonstrate a lack of belief in yourself, a lack of ambition, and a lack of confidence. You don't need to fear change. Change brings growth. So, embrace the new.

VILLAIN

The villain personality can be just as destructive as the victim. When you're the villain, you take your sadness and anger and lash out at other people. I wasted a lot of time being angry at my mom. She would call, and I wouldn't answer the phone. I would go months without seeing her. I spoke negatively about her behind her back and created a whole world and story about how awful she was. To this day I regret how much time I spent playing the villain with her. But that's the role I was playing in my story at that time.

The villain is a highly motivated, angry individual. I think villains are the most dangerous people on the planet because they spread far-reaching ripples of pain and harm. Villains often find success in leadership roles, where they continue their destructive behaviors. They can be financially well off and confident, but they operate through anger, tension, bitterness, jealousy, and the desire to oppress and mistreat others.

There can be overlap in the victim-villain personality. You're not just one thing, and you don't act just one way. From day to night, you might play different roles depending on what world you're operating in. For many years, I was a hero professionally, as a coach, but in my personal life, I often played the role of victim, and I was a villain with my mother.

Sometimes, you may be participating in the role of victim or villain unknowingly, so remember to regularly self-audit. Real mastery of your role as hero comes when you start owning every thought, feeling, and action so that you are running the show. That's true freedom.

HERO

A hero is someone who is active in their own rescue and takes responsibility for their outcome. Sometimes being the hero means pulling yourself out of a pit all by yourself, and sometimes it means seeking out the help and resources you need to succeed. You don't necessarily have to do everything all by yourself, and you should take advantage of the resources and help available to you. Ultimately, though, you are the only one responsible for your fate, and you *can* do this all by yourself if needed.

I was the victim and the villain when it came to my parents, but now I'm the hero of my story. I was able to become the hero because I owned every single thing that had occurred in my life. I owned the fact that my parents were doing the best they could. I owned the fact that losing loved ones didn't make me unique. Endings are a natural part of life. I owned the fact that my outcome is my responsibility.

Your journey will include moments of pain and suffering. You should expect it; life requires it. You're going to hurt. I don't know when your heart will be broken, but it will be broken. I don't know at what point you're going to be uncomfortable, challenged, and rejected, but it will happen.

At these times, life requires that we "play hurt." This is part of being a hero. In sports, sometimes you'll be sore, exhausted, and injured, but you have to keep playing anyway. Life is the same way. When you get knocked down, you still have to wake up every day and *do* and *be* and *exist* in this world, regardless of the tragedies or traumas you may have experienced. You still have to participate.

At times in your life, you will play the roles of victim and villain, but neither of those roles is your true identity. You were born to be the hero. When you embrace yourself as hero, you can accept your adversity, and your body, mind, and spirit will fall into perfect alignment.

NEW DEFINITION OF ADVERSITY

To accept your pain, you must find new ideas, new definitions, and new ways of thinking. That's how you change anything—by replacing old belief systems with new, more empowering ones. We don't talk about pain, discomfort, and adversity enough. It's not enough to put a label on pain and then tell someone, "Suck it up," or "Get tougher," or "That's just how it is." Yes, you will have to play hurt sometimes, but that's not the same as sucking it up and *ignoring* your pain. We need more vocabulary and a better definition of adversity to help us make sense of what's going on.

I define adversity as *law*. It is inevitable—the natural order of things. Bad things will happen to good people. Just as you will have happy moments, you will have sad moments, too. It is *normal* to lose loved ones, to struggle, to feel pain.

Nobody's going to leave this life without experiencing something uncomfortable. In an interview, Larry King asked neuropsychologist George Pratt, "What makes one person smarter than another?" Dr. Pratt answered, "Their ability to accept and adapt."

Instead of viewing adversity as an obstacle, see it as *an opportunity to grow*. The key to success is being able to take pain or a traumatic situation and still create a new path. As author Ryan Holiday says with the title of one of his books, "The obstacle is the way." Your obstacle—your adversity—is your new path. My journey now includes being adopted, being sexually abused, losing loved ones, and witnessing gun violence, and I can't simply escape that journey.

Bad things happen to good people, and good people sometimes make bad decisions. Bad decisions don't make you a bad person. Sometimes we're too hard on ourselves when we make mistakes, and we don't forgive ourselves. As I mentioned in the previous chapter, guilt and shame can hold you back. Not forgiving yourself can be as bad as being hurt by someone.

Self-forgiveness can take a long time. I struggled to forgive myself after my DUI, but that bad decision doesn't make me a bad person. I'm still not proud of my DUI, but by recognizing it as an important part of my journey, I've been able to grow, move on, and forgive myself. Today, I can use it as an advantage.

Human error must be considered when we discuss adversity in our lives. We're all human, and nobody's perfect. You'll get your feelings hurt. Someone will say the wrong thing; someone will abuse their position of authority; someone will make a bad decision on your behalf; someone will stab you in the back. And you might do all of those things to someone else. We're all humans trying the best we can with all of our adverse situations.

Most people are afraid of pain. They want to avoid it at all costs, but then they end up living lives they don't want to live. They don't take risks. They don't fall in love. They don't take the job they want. They are restricted by their fears. As we learn to discuss adversity with the right vocabulary in our own lives, we can be released from our fears and empowered to accept ourselves.

ACCEPTING PAIN MEANS ACCEPTING YOURSELF

The definition of *accept* is "to take something willingly, to endure without protest." There is no resistance when you accept. There's a willingness. You must *embrace* all that you are. You must love yourself completely, pain included, and not allow circumstances to define you. The internal self—the "I am"—is the greatest thing walking this earth.

We're not like any other creature in nature. We have the ability to control our outcomes. We've been created with self-awareness, imagination, a conscience, and a will. When you don't accept your pain, you're fighting against it. You tense up, and it feels like you're holding on so tight. Your life isn't flowing like a river as it should.

Society pulls a trick on us when it makes us think that we should be perfect or that perfection exists. It doesn't. There's no such thing as perfect. We've all done things we're not proud of. We've all been victims at one point in time.

You can't be perfect, and you don't need to be. You simply need to be yourself.

ACCEPTING PAIN UNLEASHES ENERGY TO MOVE FORWARD

Oprah said, "Forgiveness is letting go of the idea that the past should have been any different." I found the fabric of my story in that new definition of forgiveness, and it changed the way I viewed things. I thought, *Wow. If that's true forgiveness—just letting go of the idea that it should have been any different—then I can fully embrace all that I am. I can forgive the people who hurt me. I can forgive the adversity—all the circumstances and events that were out of my control. I can embrace all that has happened to me and all that I have done.*

When you accept your pain, you are no longer locking away aspects of yourself. You are working with your full potential. Your pain transforms into an energy when you know that there was a reason for your pain and that everything happened as it was supposed to.

It has been scientifically proven that humans grow most rapidly through suffering. Adversity forces us into discovery. When things are good, you're not actively looking for something more. When things are painful, you are cracked open and vulnerable. That allows you to make huge strides and drastic improvements.

I believe everything that has happened *to* me has happened *for* me. I am who I am because of what has happened—every circumstance and situation. I would not be *me* without my past adversity. Nobody else has my unique journey, and I embrace my uniqueness. I'm proud that I was adopted. I'm proud that I was a basketball player. I'm even proud that I was sexually abused.

I know that's a bold statement. But if I hadn't been sexually abused, I wouldn't be writing this book today. I wouldn't have been able to connect so strongly with the young women I coached who also suffered abuse. Because of my experience, I have been able to offer them guidance and support. I have stopped focusing on "how things should have been" and have instead accepted the reality of being sexually abused. That acceptance has given me the power and strength to help others.

You may look at your adversity and think, *How could you possibly say that terrible, traumatizing thing was* for *me? How could that be a* good *thing?*

Obviously, sexual abuse is a horrible thing. There's no question about that. Murder is a horrible thing. Alcoholism and drug addiction are horrible things. Accepting your pain does not make what happened to you good. At the same time, you can't change what has already happened. Accepting your pain means accepting that these bad things are now a part of your journey and that it is up to you to make something good from them—like lemonade from lemons. It may take time, even years, and it may take lots of work. But as the author of your story, your job is to take all the terrible, shitty things that have happened and turn them into something beautiful. Everything happens for a reason. Your job is to find that reason.

As long as you are saying, "This is such a bad thing. This shouldn't have happened to me," then you're still the victim. When you truly accept your pain, you shift to, "This happened to me, and I can't change it. This is a part of my story. I love myself and my story, so I must accept this thing, too. How can I turn it to good?" At that point, you can move into research, discovery, and openness, and you can begin the next step of the refuse-to-lose process: rewriting your story.

I look at Oprah Winfrey as a great example. She poured the energy of her pain into being a good student. She became a book lover, and she began to receive validation from her teachers because of her reading ability and articulate speech for her age. Eventually, Oprah went on to become the first self-made female black billionaire, despite growing up in poverty in rural Mississippi, suffering sexual abuse, being black, and being a woman. I truly believe that wouldn't have happened without her early adversity.

Your experience doesn't have to be that dramatic. What if you embraced your pain enough to help your family and others live better lives? You may have no idea why a traumatic event came into your space, but it did. When you accept what happened and share your story, you are able to inspire others.

Deep pain and suffering—the kind that seems to break you open and shake your entire world—will open you up in a way that other people aren't being opened. I've coached kids who lost parents at a young age. There's a depth to that kind of pain. In accepting the pain in my life, I have had to go into places in my spirit that lay dormant for years. I believe in the law of polarity, that everything has a negative and a positive. If there's an up, there's a down. If there's a hot, there's a cold. If there's sadness, there's happiness. And so, I believe that the intensity of pain on the negative side has a matching force on the positive side if we harness the energy of that pain for our personal growth.

I believe that everything is energy. Happiness is energy. Love is energy. Pain is energy. Right now, the energy of your pain might be working against you. It might be suffocating you, holding you down. Once you embrace your pain and decide to make your adversity your advantage, that energy doesn't disappear. Your shifting mindset transforms the energy into something that can work for you.

Stephen Covey said, "Pain drives openness, humility, and a desire to make improvement." In his book *Seven Habits of Highly Effective People*, he talks about the four unique human endowments: self-awareness, imagination, conscience, and independent will. We all have these gifts, and they make it possible to own and use our pain in a positive way.

Self-awareness allows you to acknowledge your pain. Then imagination helps you find new, creative definitions for adversity and what it means to your journey. Imagination also allows you to rewrite your story, which we will explore in the next chapter. Imagination lets you assign new meanings to past events and create a new life moving forward. Your conscience functions as your compass, alerting you to what is "right" and "wrong" in your life and guiding you in how to rewrite your story. Independent will is your ability to make choices. It's the desire to want and chase after more. It's the voice inside that says, *I don't want to be sad all the time. I don't want to be a prisoner to my old paradigm. I want to be free of the things limiting me.* You've already exercised independent will simply by picking up this book.

ACCEPT IT

Pain is the basis for growth and discovery. When you stop fighting against your pain and instead accept it as a part of your journey and thus a part of *you*, you will unlock your full potential.

There is a magic behind your pain. You may have to dig to find it, but the magic is there, and it can become your greatest asset.

REWRITE YOUR STORY

If your subconscious mind is going to change, for the better or the worse, it's going to happen in one of three ways.

First, an authority figure might come in and force you to adopt certain behaviors or follow a certain structure. For example, in elementary school your parents might have forced you to sit down each night and do your homework until you developed the habit yourself. We're taught from an early age to submit to leadership, our elders, and those in positions of authority. Our conditioning tells us that in every situation, someone is in charge and we should follow them. Thus, authority figures—parents, teachers, executives, political leaders, servicemen, police officers, celebrities, pastors, and the like—have the power to control how others think, feel, and act.

The second way your subconscious mind might be altered is through a personal experience of emotional impact—some life-changing event that triggers an immediate shift in your paradigm. It could be something as far-reaching and catastrophic as 9/11, or it could be more personal to you, like the death of a parent. For me, I experienced a shift following my mother's death. I grew up tremendously through that entire experience and became a better version of myself. Emotional impact can go both ways, though, as I saw firsthand with my negative reaction to my grandmother's death.

The final way to reprogram your subconscious is through constant, spaced repetition of new ideas and information. It's important to know that fighting your existing reality or your past circumstances doesn't serve you. Resistance and abundance can't exist in the same space. The beauty of your new story will make the old story obsolete.

You typically don't have control over the first two ways, so you must master the third method, which is what rewriting your story is all about.

Rewriting your story is where you own your outcome. This is where you decide, *I get one life; I get one "at bat" at this thing.* We're not on this earth long. Days turn into weeks, weeks turn into months, and months turn into years. Before you know it, decades have gone by. You don't have forever, so you must wake up and feel a sense of urgency to be free.

I really like that word—*free*—because that's what rewriting your story feels like. I'm not held back by sexual abuse or by a verbally abusive home or by the death of my grandmother. I'm owning my own story, and I'm giving these events new meaning. I'm living, day to day, exactly how I want to live. I'm living in the energy, feeling, and vibration that I want, which is love, peace, happiness, acceptance, and abundance, all of which will eventually manifest in my physical world.

It is *my* story—I am the author, the architect, the one responsible. I'm creating this thing, and I'm going to write it exactly how I want it.

Rewriting your story is about altering your self-image and self-identity—the stories you tell yourself about yourself. That is the big story: "I am this. I am that." Changing your self-image is incredibly powerful, because our bodies are an instrument of the mind. Whatever we think and feel about ourselves is what we manifest into the physical world. Rewriting your story, starting with your thoughts, will transform your life.

NOT SMART, NOT PRETTY, NOT LOVABLE: MY NEGATIVE SELF-IMAGE

I was born on May 1, 1980, in the military town of Jacksonville, North Carolina, just forty-five minutes from where I now live, in Wilmington, North Carolina. I was put up for adoption at birth and lived the first three months of my life in an orphanage before my parents, Truman and Joretta Harris, adopted me. Before me, they'd adopted my brother, Jamel, who is four years older than me. Jamel had begged for a little sister. I don't know if that was the spark that joined our four-member family, but I don't believe in randomness or coincidence. I've heard that coincidence is God's way of remaining anonymous.

I don't have any memories of my parents being together. They were separated shortly after my adoption and were legally divorced when I was three years old. At that point, my father disappeared from my life. I have to believe that, in most cases, when parents leave their children's lives, whether it be emotionally, physically, or both, somewhere in their hearts they've made a decision to do so. My father always paid his child support, but his sense of fatherly obligation was primarily limited to the financial realm, or whatever the state of North Carolina determined my brother and I were worth, but only until we turned eighteen. When my brother and I were younger, we would spend half a day with him on Christmas, and he showed up at a few graduations, but I never felt as if he wanted to have a relationship with me. Today, he is more stranger than father to me.

Due to cervical cancer, a diagnosis received in her early twenties, my mother could not bear her own children, but she had always wanted to have a house full of kids. Perhaps she desired a feeling of significance and love? In any case, in addition to adopting my brother and me, my mother fostered at least fifty kids.

I truly believe my mother had good intentions and wanted to help as many children as she could, but while I can't speak for anyone else, 2023 Briarcliff Drive was a source of significant trauma for me. Seeds were planted in that house that reaped a painful harvest.

All people have basic needs, as detailed in Maslow's hierarchy of needs.

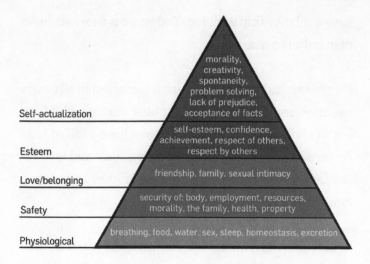

Maslow's hierarchy separates our basic needs into five categories:

- Physiological: food, water, warmth, rest
- Safety: security, safety, stability
- Love and belonging: intimate relationships—the chance to receive and give love, appreciation, and friendship
- Esteem: prestige and feeling of accomplishment
- Self-actualization: achievement of one's full potential, including creative activities, purpose, and meaning

For as much as she wanted kids, my mother wasn't a nurturer, and for me, our home wasn't safe, loving, or a place where I felt belonging or esteem. To her credit, she did always provide for my physiological needs. I always had a roof over my head and food to eat. She also always encouraged me to follow my dreams, and she gave me perhaps the greatest gift of my life by introducing me to Christ. I would not be who I am today without my faith and the drive to follow my dreams, so in a way, she helped me achieve the final step in Maslow's hierarchy of needs— self-actualization. I didn't realize it at the time, but she *was* giving me things I needed. She just wasn't giving me *everything* I needed and wanted.

For a long time, I didn't have the language to define my relationship with my mother, but now I understand that my mother was a bully. She was verbally abusive, tearing me down when I needed to be built up. She would tell me I wasn't pretty, wasn't smart, wasn't good enough. Especially in public and around other people, she would pick on me. "Why don't you tell 'em your times tables, since you've got such a smart mouth?" she'd say, knowing I struggled in math.

She never complimented me, and the first time I heard my mother tell me she loved me was when I was a freshman in college. I stored away in my mind a list of all the things she didn't like about me, and I also subconsciously downloaded the energy in which she communicated her dislike. I defined myself by those criticisms. The things she didn't like about me were the things that became personal insecurities. I still have psychological issues around math. The use of degrading language and tone is a seed planted deeply in my subconscious.

When advising me on how to handle conflict outside of our home, she encouraged me to believe in the phrase "Sticks and stones may break my bones, but words will never hurt me." As a result, I grew up thinking that neither her words nor anyone else's should hurt me, but they did, which only made me feel worse about myself. Words are powerful. They can become a part of our language and belief systems, and thus they can shape who we are.

With my father's absence and my mother's lack of nurturing, I wrote a negative story that left deep, lasting scars on my self-identity.

RECOGNIZING NEGATIVE STORIES AND REWRITING

Negative stories come from not acknowledging, accepting, and embracing your pain. These negative stories quickly become self-limiting beliefs and ideals.

I internalized my pain as part of my story. I began to believe that I had to earn love, that I wasn't smart, that I wasn't pretty, that I should be ashamed of my body, that I wasn't good enough. I didn't feel like this all the time. In fact, much of the time I felt confident and secure in my identity, especially in the world of basketball. However, because of all my insecurities around acceptance—due to my adoption, my experiences with constant loss and abandonment, my mother's emotional abuse, and my father's absence—I struggled with rejection. Rejection was a trigger for me. When faced with rejection or criticism, I would spiral into my negative self-image and begin to think and act from a place of feeling worthless.

When I began playing basketball on the collegiate level, the one thing that I'd always been good at, the thing that had been my platform for acceptance and attention, became more difficult. Basketball was supposed to be my place of security, the place where I was always good enough. It was how I'd "earned" love in my life. Because of this, putting me in a basketball environment and then telling me I wasn't good enough was a recipe for disaster.

I always wanted to be better and was willing to work for it, but without relationship coaching, I took criticism related to basketball very hard. Whenever my college coach chose not to put me in a game or embarrassed me in practice in front of my teammates—both common occurrences in sports—I internalized it to the nth degree. That same interaction would be a small thing for another teammate, but it was massive for me. It triggered a deep pain that I didn't know existed within me. I saw my coach's decision to not play me in a game or to criticize and embarrass me in front of my teammates as a personal statement about who I was—someone who wasn't good enough. My response to this lack of acceptance was the beginning of my anxiety and panic attacks. One moment I would be fine, and then it would be like the faucet had been turned on full blast. As I had done my whole life, I kept all of this bottled up inside, but each time I was triggered, the bucket inside of me grew more and more full. Eventually, all the negative emotions built up so much that they began to spill over, contributing to my thoughts of suicide and intense feelings of loneliness and depression in my college years.

Now, when I look back, I realize I had such intense reactions because my coach was an African American woman and an authority figure. In my mind, she represented a mother figure, but she ended up like my adoptive mother, who had criticized me endlessly, and my birth mother, who had me but didn't want me. Because I hadn't learned to embrace my pain and rewrite my story, I was playing the role of victim—broken child subconsciously looking for approval and love, particularly from African American women and black people in leadership positions. I wanted a mother and father that loved me, and since I couldn't get that in my home, I tried to get it from the other authority figures in my life who looked like me. My coach's intentions were just to coach me; she couldn't know that I was holding her responsible for also nurturing me through my past wounds like a mother would.

Your belief system will manifest itself in physical form in your life. The big story you tell yourself will infect your thoughts, and those thoughts will affect the way you interact with people in your day-to-day world. Just look at the harmful dynamic between many police officers and black men. That is toxic energy emerging and resurfacing out of long-held belief systems. You can see this same toxic energy in your own life when you overreact to what should be a minor issue. When you encounter a trigger like this, your pain magnifies something small and makes it seem larger and more important than it should be, causing you to look for things that aren't there or operate from assumptions. You might recognize this pattern in relationships; you meet a great guy or girl, but you act out of your past, letting your insecurities and baggage from previous relationships affect your current situation.

If you don't rewrite your story—if you don't acknowledge your pain, accept it, and then make the decision to rewrite its role in your story—then you will continue to live out your limiting beliefs. The negative story you tell yourself will show up again, and again, and again. We don't get what we want; we get who we are. You can want to be a good father, you can want to be a success in your career, you can want to be interdependent instead of codependent in your relationships. You can want, want, want, but until you *become* what you want, it won't manifest.

These negative, unhealthy stories make us "wash, rinse, and repeat" past events. They hamper our potential and prevent us from taking risks. Stories such as *I'm not smart enough, I'm not good enough, Women can't become leaders,* and *Black people never get opportunities* will hold you back. If you don't believe you can do something, you won't see the option as a possibility and will never even try. As Dr. George Pratt said in an interview with Larry King, "You cannot outperform your self-image." Until you can learn to get out of your own way, you won't be able to rise to your full potential.

Luckily, we have the ability to change negative stories. Twenty years ago, when I graduated high school, there were no women entrepreneurs, or at least very few that were well-known. It was not what women did. Now, the rate of women entrepreneurs—particularly for minority women—has been growing rapidly, and business and political opportunities for women across all industries are rapidly increasing. Now is the best time in American history to be a woman. A new story is being written. Negative stories can become a cycle, but if you proactively change the narrative, you can break the cycle—whether in your own personal life or even collectively.

TRANSFORMING NEGATIVE STORIES INTO POSITIVE ONES

We tell ourselves a story about everything. Everything is an assumption. Nothing, in reality, is "real" or "fake." Everything is filtered through our perspective. We have a belief system, and that belief system manifests into our physical world. Once you understand this, you can rewrite your negative stories into positive ones, working either backward or forward.

I would first encourage you to look backward at your past and find your pain points. Now look for the positive instead of the negative. At times, my mother made me feel like I wasn't smart or pretty, but she also *chose* me. She adopted me and picked me as her daughter. The foster children I grew up with often added to the dysfunction in my home, and constantly bonding with people only to have them disappear from my life was emotionally difficult. At the same time, interacting with so many different types of people at a young age helped make me a better communicator. I developed an ability to connect with just about everyone, and that ability has helped me as a coach, where I worked with kids from all kinds of homes, as a public speaker, and as an author. I have a unique gift to connect to the masses because of my childhood experiences. My experiences qualify me in ways others aren't, and I believe that the same is true for you.

It's easy to look at only the negative aspects of adversity, but if you're only highlighting the bad, that is all you will manifest in your life. As long as I had a negative story of my life, my thoughts and feelings would limit me. When you can create thoughts that make you feel good, your actions will soon follow. As Oprah has said, we can always choose another thought, but choosing positive thoughts instead of negative ones may be the hardest work you'll do. As Wallace D. Wattles says in *The Science of Getting Rich*:

> You have the natural inherent power to think what you want to think, but it requires far more effort to do so than it does to think the thoughts which are suggested by appearances. To think according to appearances is easy. To think truth, regardless of appearances is laborious and requires the expenditure of more power than any other work you have to perform.

> There is no labor from which most people shrink as they do from that of sustained and consecutive thought, it is the hardest work in the world.[3]

There is a connection between your unique gifts and talents and your upbringing. If you're a loving person, good at a particular sport, or an entrepreneur or if you

---

3   Wallace D. Wattles, *The Science of Getting Rich*, chapter 4 (Holyoke, MA: Elizabeth Towne Company, 1910).

cook well or if you're a great singer, where did that talent come from? Those gifts were likely nurtured in your environment. Gaining an appreciation for that upbringing—adversities and all—can provide you with a more grateful perspective.

I also encourage you to look forward. When you are on your deathbed, what do you want to leave behind? What do you want your legacy to be? Perhaps you want to have a happy, loving family or a successful career or both. Make that a part of your story now. Then you can begin to make the decisions that will lead to creating the life you want to live. Live *from* your desired outcome.

At some point, you must stop giving power to the past. Most people are addicted to their problems. They specialize in suffering because it gives them an excuse to underachieve. They fail to realize that the most successful people don't have fewer problems; they simply choose to live life on their terms. Your life is not a foregone conclusion. You have the power to change your outcome.

OWN YOUR OUTCOME

Rewriting your story means owning your outcome. You must draw a line in the sand and say, "No more. I decide from here on out who I am and who I aspire to be."

As mentioned earlier, you get to decide what role you play in the story you tell yourself: victim, villain, or hero. You must become the hero. Nothing happens without a decision, and this first decision is crucial. Decide, *I'm going to step up and own my outcome. I'm going to be the hero of my story. I don't need anyone to come save me.*

In his book *The Power of Awareness*, Neville Goddard wrote, "Everything depends upon its attitude towards itself; that which it will not affirm as true of itself cannot awaken in its world. That is, your concept of yourself, such as 'I am strong,' 'I am secure,' 'I am loved,' determines the world in which you live."

If you don't think you're worthy of love, you will not have love. If you don't adopt new beliefs as your self-image and identity—if you don't think you're strong or smart or that you can be financially free and spiritually free—then those beliefs can't manifest into your world in physical form.

Even if you don't know your goal, you can start to take responsibility for the outcome. I often hear people say they don't know what they're good at. I've always been very spoiled because I passionately and deeply loved the game of basketball for a long time, so my North Star was always very clear to me. I knew my objectives and the goal of my energies and attention. That might not be the case for you, and that's okay. You don't need to know exactly what your purpose is in life to begin rewriting your story and changing your view of yourself.

We all aspire to be strong, confident individuals. We all want joy and to live in a peaceful home. We all aspire to be someone who is not in a dark place and who is not dreading every second of the day. We all want to add value to others' lives and create a positive ripple effect in the world. In Chapter 6, "State Your Cause," I will talk more about how to identify your purpose and unique talents, but you don't necessarily need particular goals at this stage. Focus instead on these broad, universal goals: happiness, contribution, and peace.

In my opinion, becoming an incredible human being is a full-time job. That job never ends, because we are created to grow and expand in every second of the day. Even when we sleep, our brains don't stop working. You may not be able to perceive it, but you are constantly growing. At this moment, your nails are growing, your hair is getting longer, your skin is shedding, and your body is healing itself, digesting, and recovering.

Just as your physical body is always changing, you are always growing emotionally and spiritually. You are growing in your relationships, in your career, and in your self. You are either growing in the direction of who you've always been or in the direction of who you want to become. Your spirit is infinite, and thus your growth is limitless too. You are an energy force that is moving and vibrating through this world. Your job is to continue to grow, expand, and flow in unison with your greatness, or your best self. When you fight against that flow, you get sick. Stress and anxiety show up, and disease sets in. When you instead swim with the current, you will unlock your full potential.

HOW TO START UNLEARNING AND RELEARNING

To own your outcome, champion the importance of empowering questions. Ask yourself:

- Am I blaming, complaining, or defending my behavior? If so, why?
- What story am I telling myself about what's going on? Is this story helping me become the hero?
- Are my thoughts, feelings, and actions helping me own my outcome?
- What is this situation here to teach me?

Using the insights you gain from these questions, you can begin working to unlearn your environmental programming and relearn new ways of thinking and behaving.

The idea of "unlearning" may sound impossible, but it

shouldn't scare you. As you relearn and adopt new ideas and information, unlearning happens naturally. Gradually, you move out of old thought patterns and into new ways of thinking and operating.

To unlearn and relearn information, it helps to understand how your brain works. A basic knowledge of neuroscience will help you know and understand yourself better, allowing you to implement new strategies and techniques that will accelerate your growth and help you own your outcome. I believe the world's best teacher of this information is Bob Proctor. Bob has been teaching people how to shift their paradigm for over fifty years, and I've been a student of his for about ten of those fifty years.

First, you should understand that we have both a conscious mind and a subconscious mind, which both influence the body, or your actions. Bob represents this with his famous stick person diagram:

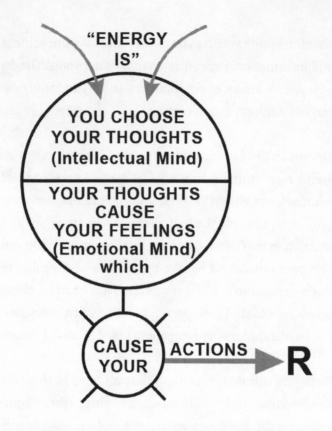

The conscious mind is the thinking brain. It's the part of us that accepts, rejects, and imagines information, and it includes our five sensory learning systems—sight, sound, smell, touch, and taste. Information arrives into our five senses, and our conscious mind processes it.

From birth to age six, we cannot reject anything that comes in through those five sensory learning systems. So when you're two years old, you cannot reject sounds you hear or foods you eat or what you see. You can only accept the information you receive and download it into your system as truth, which becomes your belief system.

From the ages of six to nine, we can only reject about a third of what we take in through our senses. This is why kids easily believe in Santa Claus and the tooth fairy and why I thought that if I put a cape on and jumped off the top of the house, I would fly, just like Superman.

However, the conscious mind is open to logic and reason, and once we mature, it is able to analyze the information given to it and determine the validity and importance of that information. Eventually, we realize that Santa Claus isn't real.

The subconscious mind is the feeling brain. It works twenty-four hours a day. I like to think of my subconscious mind as my soul. When you go see your favorite singer perform live, the experience is different than listening to him or her on the radio. The overall experience is enhanced. That's kind of how the subconscious and conscious minds are different—the subconscious holds your deepest emotional and spiritual memories.

The issue with the subconscious mind is that it only accepts. It lacks the capacity to reject anything; it accepts all information fed to it, unable to discern real from fake. This is dangerous, especially since some of us grew up in toxic environments. We experience abuse and an upbringing without love or belonging, and our subconscious mind automatically records and remembers that. The resulting downloaded paradigms and beliefs affect how we view the world as adults.

Typically, we don't recognize until we're twenty to twenty-five that we have toxic paradigms. Once we realize we have a problem, we can begin to identify the thoughts and behaviors we don't like through asking ourselves empowering questions, but it's not always easy to put an end to those thoughts and behaviors, because they are embedded in our subconscious minds. Our body is the instrument of our mind, and it performs and acts out whatever is in the subconscious mind.

In an interview, Dr. George Pratt said that the conscious mind fires twenty to forty neurons a second, while the subconscious mind fires twenty to forty *million* neurons a second. In other words, the subconscious mind is a million times more powerful than the conscious mind. Dr. Pratt described the relationship between conscious mind and subconscious mind as that between a flea and an elephant. If a flea is riding on an elephant's back and the elephant decides to go for a walk, then that flea is going to go for a walk, too!

It sounds like you're at the mercy of your subconscious,

right? Essentially, you are. Your subconscious mind is powerful. You have been hardwired to think, feel, and act in certain ways. Fortunately, the subconscious mind's greatest weakness is also its greatest strength: it will accept whatever you put into it. That means you can train your subconscious. It takes time, but if you keep putting in new, positive thoughts, images, sounds, and information, you will eventually begin shifting your programmed beliefs in a positive direction. You can't make the negative stuff disappear, but you can shift your focus, concentrating solely on thoughts that empower you, celebrate you, encourage you, and inspire you.

UNLEARNING AND RELEARNING

It is absolutely critical to unlearn harmful environmental programming—any downloaded paradigms we adopted from our parents, family, friends, school, church, and community that are responsible for a mindset of limitation or lack. These are belief systems that cause anxiety, worry, and stress, and when left unattended, they prevent us from fully expressing ourselves and maximizing our full potential. This in turn can cause anger, depression, and disease.

Your expectations of yourself come from your downloaded paradigms. Your paradigms have almost exclusive control over your habitual behavior, and the huge bulk of our behavior is habitual. We almost always do what comes naturally, which is why it's critical to develop strong, healthy paradigms of love, self-acceptance, confidence, abundance, and joy.

From our birth, expectations are placed on us by others without our permission or consent. These expectations are based on other people's paradigms and generations-old belief systems, and they can reach into any aspect of our life. For example, a young person might wonder whether they are allowed to be gay while also having a relationship with God. They might think, *My parents said I couldn't, and my church said the same, so I don't think I can.* You might wonder whether you are allowed to date outside your race. You might wonder whether someone like you, from a small town or village in the middle of nowhere, can live your dreams.

If someone puts expectations on you before you can say who you want to be, then you risk living your life according to their expectations. The truth is, human beings have been offering their personal opinions on things—opinions based solely on their programming—for centuries. In some cases, this will benefit you, and in others, this is how cycles of limiting beliefs can span across generations. I often have to remind myself that at some point, someone decided that black people shouldn't be allowed to vote or share facilities with white people because they were seen as less human than their white peers. The goal was to disempower an entire group of people in order to ensure the power of another. Who actually believed this stuff? Oh yeah, former US presidents, governors, mayors—nearly everyone in a leadership position. We must question old, outdated ways of thinking. Otherwise, we let others' beliefs define what's possible for us.

In 2016, a man who was recorded saying "I just grab 'em by the pu**y" (in reference to his strategy for picking up women) was elected as the forty-fifth president of the United States. This is a great example of paradigms and old belief systems that no longer work. I would think that no woman would vote for a man who sexually violates women, but nearly half of white women voted in his favor. To me, two things made this happen: these women's voting paradigm was "Republican," and their paradigm concerning white men's sexual assault against women was "Boys will be boys."

However, Trump's election forced a lot of people to question these old paradigms. I believe the statement "grab 'em by the pu**y," combined with Trump securing the presidency, led to the greatest women's movement our country has ever known. The 2017 #MeToo and Time's Up movements would not exist if Tarana Burke and Christy Haubegger (key leaders in #MeToo and Time's Up, respectively) didn't question our country's outdated beliefs around the subject of sexual violence toward women. Likewise, without the questioning of old belief systems, the record-breaking number of women that ran for office in 2018 and won would not have been possible:

> Already in 2018, women candidates have broken the records for the number of candidates for governor, U.S. House, and U.S. Senate. And that trend continued in the 2018 midterm elections.

> The U.S. House of Representatives elected a record number of women, with at least 90 women expected to make their way to Washington, D.C. in January.[4]

Understanding the way the mind works and how we arrive at our beliefs is key. It's important to realize that our ideas about our limits and even our self-worth come from our environments. The ability to believe you can do something is very important. Every ten-year-old child, whether male or female, black or white, rich or poor, gay or straight, should believe that they can go to college, become a doctor, own their own business, or become a member of Congress. Unfortunately, most children's beliefs reflect their environment and their parents' or grandparents' paradigms.

---

4   Samantha Cooney, "Here Are Some of the Women Who Made History in the Midterm Elections," *Time*, September 13, 2018, updated November 7, 2018, http://time.com/5323592/2018-elections-women-history-records/.

I encourage you to question your programmed belief systems. Adversity opens you up to become vulnerable and realize, *This doesn't make sense anymore. This isn't working for me.* Adversity is the catalyst to make you go back and start questioning what you've learned.

Once you identify what isn't working for you, you can unlearn your limiting paradigms and replace them with new information. For example, I have unlearned what society has taught me about being black. Race plays a huge role in our paradigms and belief systems. Society has defined all races, cultures, ages, and genders for us, and many times those definitions are limiting or harmful. Society's definition of blackness did not serve me, so I wrote my own definition.

I view being black as beautiful. It's magical, and it's proud, strong, and inspirational. From the beginning of time, we have defied the odds and fought for our seat at the table. In every industry, generations after generations have broken down barriers and pushed the culture forward. My increased awareness of my *real* black history leaves me in awe. I'm speechless when I listen to James Baldwin or Nina Simone or Maya Angelou speak. These are the voices of black excellence. I feel a responsibility to leave behind messages of meaning and purpose that elevate our culture, as they have. By unlearning society's limiting picture of being black and replacing it with my own paradigm, my blackness has become one of my greatest strengths.

To "unlearn," you replace old information with lots of new, accurate information, thus rendering the old information obsolete. If you want to lose weight, you don't forget that fried food is tasty; you just gain new information about how to eat tasty, healthy meals. New ideas, new meanings, new thoughts, new actions, all applied and repeated, render old habits and old ideas obsolete. That is how you begin reprogramming your subconscious and rewriting your story.

Part of this process requires relearning. Relearning allows you to make the transition from being victim or villain to hero. In the process of relearning, you can unlearn the damaging paradigms that have been downloaded into your subconscious.

You should begin your relearning work by focusing on improving your ways of thinking, and then your ways of behaving will follow suit.

WAYS OF THINKING

So, you've decided that you want to change your story. At this point, through self-auditing and self-awareness, you should have an idea of what your current self-image is, and you should know what you want your self-image to be instead. Remember: it's okay if you don't have all the details figured out. Maybe you don't know your purpose or exactly what you want out of life, but you know that you want to be more confident. That's enough.

To rewrite your story, you must intentionally feed your conscious and subconscious minds with information matching your desired new self-image. *Intentionally* is the key word here. Your story isn't going to rewrite itself; you must actively work to make this happen.

For example, I am intentional in that I wake up in the morning and write out ten things that I'm grateful for. I communicate out loud who I am and write a self-confidence formula every day. I keep a goal card with my most important goals concretely written out. I surround myself with self-image identity pieces (like my vision boards, which I will discuss later). I am even intentional in my own thoughts. My mind is my greatest tool, so I carefully control my thoughts. I don't leave the doors of my mind open to things that shouldn't be there, like negativity and self-doubt.

The mind is a garden, and if you don't tend to it daily by nurturing, watering, weeding, and protecting it, then negative thoughts can run right through it. You are responsible for envisioning the person you want to be—

to write it out, to communicate it out loud, to make it known to yourself. You are responsible for monitoring your thoughts and gently guiding yourself back to more positive attitudes when you feel yourself veering into negativity and doubt.

Your new objective is to live the best version of yourself every day. That's difficult, but with daily practice, being the best version of yourself becomes easier and even fun. Whatever new self-image you desire, you must hold it in your mind and focus all of your attention and energy into that new identity.

You should aim to make sure the information you take in through your five senses supports your new story. It won't always be possible, but when you can, remove yourself from situations that don't support your new story. For instance, if you want to have a more positive attitude and one of your friends is always negative, spend less time with him or her.

If you can't remove yourself from the situation, focus on rewriting your story in the moment. Let's say you're trying to become more confident and your boss criticizes you at work. You may be tempted to spiral into self-doubt, but instead, strive to approach the situation with confidence. Remind yourself that even successful people make mistakes, and tell yourself that you are getting better and better. Despite any particular event or circumstance, you are always responsible for the thoughts you think.

To rewrite your ways of thinking, you must address your attitudes about the world and your circumstances.

Rewriting your own self-image will take you far, but there are some things about yourself you cannot change. I am black, and I have been sexually abused. Those things aren't going to change, no matter how much I rewrite my story. So I've needed to relearn new beliefs and attitudes around those truths.

Statistics say that a vast majority of sexually abused kids will not attend college. They are also more likely to suffer addiction and commit suicide. Statistics show that black people are more likely to live in poverty and are less likely to achieve corporate success compared to their white counterparts. If I believe these stats, I will stay in that mindset and follow those limiting paradigms. Instead, I've replaced that narrative with a new story: a story that says sexually abused kids have unlimited potential and can achieve unimaginable greatness if they harness the energy of their pain; a story that the world respects confidence, strength, and determination more than it cares about race or childhood trauma; a story that as long as we strive to be our best selves, the universe will reward our efforts.

When you adjust your ways of thinking, your ways of behaving will naturally follow. Thoughts are transferred into feelings, which become physical things in the universe.

For this chain reaction of change to occur, your thoughts must be supported by deep belief. It may take some time for you to develop this belief. For example, wealthy people can easily say, "I live an abundant life," and believe it. The poorest person can say the same words but may not actually believe it. Only once they believe the thought will they be operating at the right frequency to attract that abundance into their life.

The repetition of the right thoughts will eventually lead to belief, which will lead to action. For example, if you want to be confident and intentionally tell yourself that you *are* confident, you will be primed to seek out confidence in your life. You will begin to identify confidence in those around you and model that behavior. You may also disassociate from the people who demonstrate a distinct lack of confidence so that you can protect your subconscious mind from their influence. In this way, as you begin to think of yourself as a confident individual, you will also begin to *behave* like a confident person.

Fill your conscious mind with intentional thoughts that

reflect your desired new story, and eventually those thoughts will take root in your subconscious mind as deep feelings. The new ideas and new thoughts, followed by a deep belief, will make the old ideas and the old thoughts obsolete. Since your subconscious drives the majority of your habitual behavior, those new feelings will become action. Change moves from the conscious to the subconscious, and then the body naturally follows.

HOW TO REWRITE YOUR STORY WITHIN

When you rewrite your story within, there's nothing external involved. In my case, it's not about me and my mom or my dad or my coach or my boss. It's about me and the commitment I make to myself every day. I have the power to think and feel whatever I want. As such, I have the power to transform my attitude and change the negative meanings I've put on my experiences.

In this process, it's important to recognize the strength you've already shown. Give yourself credit where credit is due. You have crossed hurdles and made it through difficult situations before. Seeing your past strength will encourage you. You can think, *I've done it before, and I can do it again. I know I can do this.*

The more you work any muscle, the stronger that muscle gets, and the more frequently that muscle will activate.

If you frequently work the muscle of worry, you will tend to worry more out of habit. If you instead work the muscles of confidence, certainty, faith, and belief, you will strengthen those characteristics, and they will activate more often. Like anything, with practice, things get easier, and you get better.

The more you activate your mental muscle and work on rewriting your story, the more quickly you'll be able to take future hits of adversity and spin them around to something positive. Eventually, you will get to the point where, instead of reacting without thinking, you can choose how to respond to any situation, regardless of how tragic it might be. This is an empowering place to be because you have complete control over your thoughts, feelings, and, thus, actions.

Neither theology nor science can find any limits to the human mind. A hundred years ago, nobody would have expected we'd be where we are today. African Americans and women have far more rights today, we've had a black president, gay marriage is legal, we've traveled into space, and now even self-driving cars are just around the corner. Humans go about living their lives, finding problems that need to be solved, and then creating answers. But science cannot tell us what the next thing is. There's no telling what human minds will come up with in the next hundred years.

Similarly, over the years, theologians have also upheld the limitless nature of the human mind and spirit. Bob Proctor has said that we are spiritual beings living a human experience. At times, that human experience causes us to adopt imperfect belief systems, but at our core, our spiritual DNA is perfect. We are God's greatest form of creation. We are an extension of God himself, and no weapon formed against us shall prosper. We are the recipients of a wealth of abundance, and we can achieve and become anything we desire.

There are no limits to your mind, and so you can rewrite your story any way you wish with a few different strategies I will briefly review: working on a positive mental attitude, mastering your language, using visualization, meditating, exercising, and making use of repetition. I believe a positive mental attitude, mastery of your language, and repetition are absolutely necessary to rewrite your story, but when it comes to visualization, meditation, and exercise, do what works for you. You may find that visualization just doesn't work for you, and that's okay. Trust yourself and do what will inspire you.

POSITIVE MENTAL ATTITUDE

One of the first things you must do when embarking on rewriting your story is deciding to live a life of positive meaning. Your transformation to your best self begins with a positive mental attitude.

I began to adopt a positive mental attitude in my mid-twenties. I did it because I was desperate and trying to survive. I knew I was hurting, and I wanted to figure out what to do with my anger. I didn't know what my potential was, but I wanted to be successful, and I felt something inside that wanted to be greater. Every time I read a different book or researched a different topic or studied a different person, I identified a common theme: positive mental attitude. So that's where I started.

Positive mental attitude comes down to directing your thoughts. While you often cannot directly control your subconscious mind, you can control the thoughts of your conscious mind. It's a little like training a dog. At first, you must keep the dog on a leash, or it might run out into the street, where it can get hurt. With enough training, though, the dog will stay by your side even without the leash. Similarly, by directing your conscious thoughts to a positive mental attitude, you will train your subconscious to do the same.

You're not going to wake up one morning and suddenly have a positive mental attitude. You must *choose* it, deliberately and intentionally, and you must continue to choose it each day. I began working on my own positive mental attitude over a decade ago, and I am still committed to working on it today.

The key to directing your thoughts is mastering your language. It's toxic to speak negatively about ourselves, our journey, and our experiences. We should be our biggest fans. Our job is to champion our story. To be the hero. To stand up with the sword and say, "We are going over the hill to fight anything coming our way." Our job is not to sit back and talk negatively about who we are. "I'm too fat. I'm not smart enough. I can't do that." That's not our job. Enough people out in the world will already do that for us.

Part of mastering language is stopping the negative self-talk, and part of it is consciously using positive language. One way to ensure positive self-talk is to use affirmations, which I like to call statements of truth. An affirmation is defined as the action or process of affirming something or being affirmed. I believe that affirmations should be spoken in the present tense, as fact, to be the most effective. "I *am* a strong, confident woman." It's important that your statements of truth are backed up by deep emotion and belief. Take all the energy of your pain and pour it into your affirmations.

These are my statements of truth:

> I impact people's minds. I touch people's hearts. I ignite people's spirits. I don't beat myself up. I don't judge myself based on other people's point of view. I am empathetic to

others' point of view, but they are not my burden. I am the best person to solve this problem. I convey the impression of advancement with everything I do. I advance all people who deal with me. I am moving in the direction of increase, and it permeates every action. I live a life of meaning and purpose. The world needs my greatness. Nothing that I have been through cripples me. My experiences only qualify me. I am the elite in my field of public speaking and inspiration. I deeply and completely accept myself with any challenges and all my strength. I place myself in a perpetual state of preparation and discomfort because my power is beyond my comfort zone. I expect great things to happen in my life. My vision is my reality. I possess a favor mindset.

My predominant thoughts are of wealth and abundance. My predominant thoughts are of helping the world become a better place by sharing my story. My predominant thoughts are of influencing every person I meet in a positive way. I am the master of my thoughts. Only good comes into my life. I have the capacity to manifest any dream. God's wealth flows to me in avalanches of abundance. All of my needs are met instantaneously. That which I seek is seeking me. I am not at the mercy of anything. I am not hindered by anything. I am available to receiving more good than I have ever experienced, realized, or imagined in my life.

I read these statements of truth aloud every single morning because they make me feel good. That may sound like a small thing, but we all want to feel good, and when we feel optimistic and inspired, we can make positive changes in our lives. My purpose is to inspire others, so I need to have the juice when people need it. Starting my day with these affirmations reinforces the new story I've written for myself and gives me the energy I need to be my best self.

We can't ignore the importance of our words. Words create thoughts, which generate feelings, which inspire action. If our words don't make us feel good and align with our story, we should change our words.

VISUALIZATION

As humans, we have incredible imaginations, and we can visualize being and becoming anything. Remember: your subconscious mind accepts everything you give it. Visualization is incredibly powerful because your subconscious mind doesn't know if the images you create are real or fake; it just accepts them as truth. Thus, when you do visualization work, you are training your subconscious thoughts and feelings, which will then manifest into action.

I've always been a very visual person. I created my first official vision board in 2009, but even before then, I had a vision board without realizing that's what it was. My entire bedroom in middle school and high school was my vision board. Every inch of my walls, from floor to ceiling, was covered with Michael Jordan posters and newspaper clippings of Wake Forest basketball players likes Tim Duncan and Randolph Childress. I stayed in my room a lot, hiding from the things going on in my house, and in that time, the images plastered on my wall were entering my subconscious mind.

For a long time, I had no idea how I ended up at Wake Forest University, and, frankly, it still astounds me. When I was in sixth grade, one of my teachers told me that Wake Forest was where the really smart students went. I didn't get terrible grades, but I wasn't the best student in the world either. Until then, I hadn't thought about the academic part of Wake Forest; I just knew they had a great men's basketball program. My teacher's offhand comment filled me with discouraging thoughts, but despite my new doubts, I still ended up getting an opportunity to go to my dream school.

Looking back at my life now, I can see that everything was being created. Nothing is an accident. There are no coincidences. I lived off of "Tobacco Road," the only place in America where there are four major NCAA Division I basketball programs within an hour and a half of each other—Wake Forest, NC State, Duke, and the University of North Carolina. Every day I saw images of

Michael Jordan and Wake Forest on my walls and visualized myself being among the best. Every day I watched great basketball players and visualized myself joining their ranks. And my visualizations became my reality. I became a basketball player at Wake Forest, competing in what I believe to be the best basketball league ever, the Atlantic Coast Conference.

Everyone's vision board is personal. Your vision board will depend on your vision of yourself. Vision boards are a great tool because they add clarity to your mental picture. We learn in pictures and have vivid imaginations, but we don't always use our imaginations fully. Having images outside of ourselves allows us to fill in the details and make our imagined visualizations more concrete. If every day you see an image of what you want, you'll be reminded of how much you want that thing and why, thus directing your subconscious thoughts in a direction that will help manifest your desires in the physical world.

Oftentimes our biggest dreams, the ones we *really* want, scare us. We're hesitant to pursue those dreams because we're afraid of failure and disappointment. Those fears are embedded in our subconscious, but if we can visualize ourselves actually achieving those dreams, we instead ignite feelings of joy, accomplishment, and pride within our subconscious. Those feelings can give us the courage to pursue those big, scary dreams.

I started my first official vision board right after my DUI. For me, the foundation of my vision board was strong and confident women. That was who I wanted to be. So I found images of women who exemplified that ideal and put them on my board. Oprah was of course on the board.

I was also seeking to become a head coach at the time, so I included images of leaders I admired, like a picture of Barack and Michelle Obama right in the center. I had a few images related to championships on there too because, professionally, I wanted to win championships.

I like nice things and don't deny myself material pleasures, so I included images of physical things I wanted as well, like an amount of money I wanted to make, ocean-view beach houses, and a couple of Mercedes-Benz cars.

I also put inspirational text and quotes on my board, like "The dream is big. Dream bigger." I was challenging myself to expand my thinking, because limited vision keeps us small. My vision board also proclaimed, "You're reading your book. You are an author." I also included "Refuse to lose" or "RTL" on the board three different times, representing the company I wanted to create to help inspire people.

Three years after creating my vision board and beginning my work on making adversity my advantage, I had become a head coach, won four championships, tripled my income, and driven two of the cars I'd put on the board. Some of the things I put on that first vision board are just now being accomplished. I've created my Refuse to Lose company, and I've written my book. Sometimes we need to be patient, but visualizations will indeed take shape in the physical world.

I've created five new vision boards since 2009, and I have them hanging less than five feet from my bed so that I see them constantly. In this way I can continue to direct my thoughts positively. For me, my goals are literally never out of reach.

You can practice visualization in other ways besides vision boards. In sports, for example, it's helpful to visualize practices as if they are games. This ensures you are getting the most out of practice and will be prepared when game day actually arrives.

Visualization allows you to manipulate your subconscious mind, allowing you to create the life you desire and make your dreams as real as your current physical reality. If you truly believe in your dreams as though they are your physical reality, those dreams must manifest in your world. It's not luck; it's *law*.

MEDITATION

Meditation is no longer the wild, mysterious thing it once was. More and more people are recognizing its benefits, and so it is becoming a part of our culture. Celebrities like Oprah Winfrey have normalized the conversation of spiritual awareness and spiritual awakening, and meditation has been at the forefront of that conversation.

Personally, I haven't yet mastered meditation. I've just recently started doing five- to ten-minute meditations, but I've already found that it centers and balances me.

The key to meditation is being still and listening to your breath. By focusing on your breathing, you can silence or muffle the endless stream of thoughts most of us live with day in and day out, which allows you to be present and in the moment.

Meditation puts you in a relaxed state. It makes you open and clear. Most of the time, worry, stress, and anxiety cloud your other emotions and thoughts. When you are in a meditative state, your dreams, goals, ambitions, and the full vastness and purpose of yourself can come to you.

If you've never meditated before, I recommend starting with a short amount of time. I also recommend searching YouTube for video resources, especially if you're interested in guided meditation.

EXERCISE

When I was young, though I didn't realize it at the time, basketball was a form of therapy for me, and the one period of time I stopped exercising was when I was trying to drink my life away. Now, I exercise at least four to five times a week. I need exercise to feel my best.

Exercise has both physical and mental benefits, leading to a healthier body and mind. Many people exercise to lose weight or achieve a certain look. For those people, the physical results they see from exercise can make them feel stronger and more confident. Exercising also releases "feel-good" chemicals, like dopamine, in your brain, and it has been shown to help reduce stress. Exercise is our best medicine!

REPETITION

Repetition is an age-old, tried-and-true strategy for learning new information and building new habits. As Zig Ziglar said, "Repetition is the mother of learning, the father of action, which makes it the architect of accomplishment." Repetition is absolutely vital in rewriting your story, as it is how you will supplant old beliefs in your subconscious with new ones. Repetition of the right thoughts and behaviors will truly change your life.

I'm not lying when I say that I listened to the audio book

of *The Secret* for thirty days straight. I had a forty-five-minute commute to work at the time, so I put my drive to good use by religiously listening to *The Secret*, a book about the law of attraction. I also watched the Oprah DVD collection at least a hundred times. By reading and listening to the same material again and again, I was able to gain new insights that I missed the first time around.

I highly recommend, for example, that you read this book multiple times, because with each read you should gain more clarity. As you reach new points in your journey, new things will click for you. I can't count the number of times I've returned to a book or video and thought, *Oh, I get that part now! I'm ready to implement this suggestion now, and I think I can do that other thing even better at this point.* Plus, the repetition carves out grooves in the subconscious mind.

While rewriting your story gets easier with time, the work never stops completely. You must stay repetitive in what you're trying to do and what you're trying to become. Keep building a positive mental attitude, keep directing your thoughts, keep visualizing, keep meditating, keep exercising. Remember: most of our behavior is habitual. Repetition is what creates habits.

REWRITING YOUR STORY IN THE WORLD

The way you express yourself to others has a lot to do with what's happening within. If you struggle to treat people the right way, that means you still have work to do internally. Take deliberate action every day to try to look at the world in the most positive way, in a beautiful way, because the world *is* beautiful.

Just as you want to master the language you use in self-talk, you should seek to also master the language you use externally with others. If you find that you're slipping into negative language with a certain person or in a certain environment, take a step back and evaluate your role the situation.

When we slip up—whether we snap at our child in frustration or put someone down or say something hurtful to our significant other in the heat of the moment—we tend to either blame the other person or treat our emotions and behavior as byproducts of the situation. Remember, though, if you are defending your behavior, you are likely playing the role of victim or villain. Everything you think, feel, and do is a reflection of your subconscious mind. So instead of focusing on the situation or what the other person did or said, look at yourself. Ask, "Why did I respond that way? What should I be learning from this situation?"

As you work to rewrite your story in the world, you have to be stingy with your time and your attention. To live a life of purpose and freedom will require all your attention, so you must intentionally select who gets your time and energy.

This process is ultimately about you and your effort, but we're all influenced by the people around us. If the people around you aren't aligned with your goals, it's going to make your job that much harder. While you're trying to create a new story for yourself, the people around you may still be operating under your old belief system. You may have to move outside of those people to find a path for your journey that will work for you.

At the same time, surrounding yourself with people aligned with your goals can give you much-needed support. If you want to exercise more, you'll likely find it easier if you have a friend to go to the gym with you and to help hold you accountable. You could also sit down and create a vision board with someone else.

Trust yourself. We can get so concerned about what other people think and what other people are doing. The truth is, most people are not living healthy, free lives. They're not making adversity their advantage or owning their outcome. They're simply not. If you try to look to the people in your environment for validation and a pat on the back, you may not find it. Instead, you should work to find the strength and encouragement within.

Finally, make positively oriented decisions about what you do. Just as you must be intentional about *who* you spend your time with, you must be intentional about *what* you spend your time doing. Remember that everything you experience is being funneled into your subconscious mind, so spend your time doing things that will reinforce the new story you are writing for your life.

REWRITE YOUR STORY

Adversity and pain tend to lead us to write negative, limiting, and even destructive stories. Our everyday thoughts and actions are shaped by the stories we tell ourselves, so we must rewrite more-positive stories.

By rewriting your story, you enable yourself to own your outcome—you allow yourself to choose your own destiny.

MODEL OTHERS

Rewriting your story is both the starting point and a continual practice. Through constant repetition, the goal is to make your new thoughts, feelings, and behaviors habitual, a part of your lifestyle. Transformation occurs when you consistently align thought, feeling, and action so that each reinforces the others. If you fall out of alignment with just one of these, then your weakness in that area will hold you back from the exponential growth you could achieve.

I believe that to think, feel, and act as we choose is our greatest power but the hardest to master. You can't transform or change anything, though, unless you have a burning desire to change and a new story to replace the old. So where do you find the new thoughts, feelings, and actions that you want to implement? This is where modeling comes in.

You need new ideas. If you grew up poor, you need new ideas on how to become wealthy. How do you get those new ideas? You go and find wealthy people. If you need new ideas on how to become a leader, you go and find leaders. If you need new ideas on how to develop healthier communication skills, you go and find good communicators. Whatever your goals, challenges, or objectives are, whatever you want your new story to be, you've got to find people who match that story and follow their blueprint.

Romans 12:2 (KJV) says, "And be not conformed to this world: but be ye transformed by the renewing of the mind, that ye may prove what is that good, and acceptable, and perfect, will of God." Similarly, in *The Power of Awareness*, Neville Goddard said:

> To be transformed, the whole basis of your thoughts must change. But your thoughts cannot change unless you have new ideas, for you think from your ideas. All transformation begins with an intense, burning desire to be transformed. The first step in the "renewing of the mind" is *desire*.

None of your thoughts, feelings, or behaviors are unique. You learned them by modeling others, like your parents. We all naturally adopt and reflect the behaviors of other people, typically those in our immediate environment.

Modeling is going to happen regardless, with or without

your consent. The thing you *can* control is whether you mimic attitudes and behaviors that align with the new story you are writing for yourself or that keep you stuck in your current paradigm or, even worse, download habits that are far from the person you want to be. As with all the steps detailed in this book, you must be *intentional*. If you want to ensure you're modeling positive, productive attitudes and behaviors, you must consciously choose your role models and what qualities of those role models you wish to mimic in your own life.

In Chapter 3, you began rewriting your new self-identity and new lifestyle. Everything must be a map toward that identity. The models you choose fill in the details of that map, revealing the routes—the thoughts, feelings, and behaviors—that will take you to your desired destination.

ARE YOU READY FOR THE NEXT STEP?

At this point, you should want to change and to write your new story. You should have a good idea about what paradigms you want to unlearn and what you want to become. You're likely excited about the prospect of that change, but you may feel overwhelmed and unsure where to start. Maybe you just don't feel quite *ready* to take the next step of actually implementing that change in your life.

Even in the most painful situations, people return to old

behaviors because their subconscious minds are most comfortable there. People return to abusive relationships; they return to jail; they continue cycles of toxic behaviors, such as eating disorders, alcoholism, or bad spending habits. Many people are afraid of the new and don't feel "ready," so they return to old ways of thinking and never escape.

I passionately believe that people are not lazy or incapable. They're simply paralyzed by fear—fear of failure, fear of the unknown, fear of not being good enough. All of their paradigms hold them hostage. I believe we innately have a burning desire to do and become what it is that we've been put here to do, but we rationalize standing still, and we give ourselves excuses. We say, "I'm not ready. I don't have the resources I need. I don't have the time, energy, or money." Then we act victimized, and we blame, complain, and defend a life that we've created.

You simply have to take action and move forward. You're *never* going to feel ready, because readiness is a myth. You're never going to feel comfortable taking steps to do something you've never done before. Change is scary, so you're going to experience internal resistance when you try to step outside of your habitual ways of operating. You can't let fear hold you back. You only have one life to live, so you must force yourself to keep moving forward and growing.

Finding good models can help you overcome your fear. The more you learn about something, the less afraid of it you are. By seeking out models and identifying the thoughts and behaviors that helped them succeed, you will learn more about what you can do to achieve your own success. Having real-life examples and success stories gives you a roadmap to follow.

MY GREATEST MODEL: OPRAH WINFREY

To me, Oprah is like the Internet. The Internet has completely transformed our world, and it's going to be the catalyst for many new developments in the next one hundred years. It has transcended its original roots to become something infinitely powerful. Oprah is a force in our world like that.

Oprah's introduction into my life was one of my greatest watershed moments. There was before Oprah, and then there is after Oprah. Oprah came into my life at a time when I needed exactly that kind of influence, and she has been a huge, key component to my success and growth as a person. I've watched hours upon hours of her truth and her story. She was the answer to all the questions I didn't even know I had.

I cannot emphasize enough how revolutionary and courageous Oprah was to simply *be* and *share* herself in the public sphere. Oprah was one of the first people on TV to express unfiltered vulnerability. She talked openly about sexual abuse and adversity at a time when these unspoken wounds were normally swept under the rug. Before I heard Oprah put into words what sexual abuse does to a person, I felt like there was something wrong with me. I felt ashamed and guilty of the sexual abuse I'd suffered, and I felt like my resulting behavior was my fault. But then Oprah told me that sexual abuse causes people to act out in certain ways, like adopting promiscuous behavior and feeling shame and guilt.

Oprah helped me realize why I thought, felt, and acted the way I did, and her life was proof that there was a way through the adversity—a way to shed the old, limiting beliefs and come out the other side stronger.

I was drawn strongly to Oprah because my story aligns with hers in many ways. We're both black women. We both suffered sexual abuse at the age of eight and, because of it, didn't learn healthy views of sex growing up. We both had strained relationships with our mothers, feeling angry at them for not protecting us and for not being more loving and nurturing. We both found solace in our faith. When someone asked Oprah what gave her hope throughout her struggles, Oprah said that she believed God's Word that she could do all things through Christ who strengthened her. I had heard that scripture plenty of times growing up, and it had also been a beacon of hope for me.

James Baldwin said, "If you can examine and face your life, you can discover the terms with which you are connected to other lives, and they can discover them too. You read something which you thought only happened to you, and you discovered it happened 100 years ago to Dostoyevsky. This is a very great liberation for the suffering, struggling person, who always thinks they're alone."[5] That was what Oprah did for me—she showed me that I was not alone.

I was also able to look at Oprah and say, "Here is this amazing, revolutionary woman who went through so much of the same adversity that I did but who went on to experience great personal growth and success in her career. If she was able to become the strong, confident leader she is, then I can do it too."

When I first began my journey of making adversity my advantage, I didn't know exactly what to do. Oprah gave me a blueprint. I was thirsty for new ways of being, new paradigms, and Oprah was my water. She told me to journal, and I journaled. She told me to practice empathy and gratitude, and I did. I've been listening to Oprah since

---

5   James Baldwin, "An Interview with James Baldwin" [interview by Studs Terkel in 1961], *Conversations with James Baldwin* (Jackson: University Press of Mississippi, 1989).

2005, and through constant repetition, I started replacing my old programmed beliefs with the new, better beliefs that Oprah preached.

Oprah made me grow more self-aware, and she made me want to be smarter, too. I had never defined myself as smart, so that new desire was important to me. My brother was always "the smart one." I was an athlete who *could* apply herself academically but never did. Oprah has credited her intelligence—her ability to read and speak well—with being the one thing she could "hang her hat on." If it was so important to her, I wanted to cultivate that drive for knowledge in myself, too. I opened up a lot of books because of Oprah Winfrey. Anytime she recommended a resource, I devoured it.

To this day, I continue to model myself after Oprah. One of the main reasons I left my coaching career was because I wanted to share my true story, just like Oprah did before me. She showed me that it's best to be your authentic self and that you might help someone just by telling your truth. She helped me realize that we all share the same human experience.

WHERE TO FIND MODELS

Oftentimes we don't see ourselves in other people. You may look at someone else's life and assume that they're completely different from you. I could have looked at Oprah and thought, *She's far more talented than I am. I'll never be that successful.* However, just because someone's *doing* better than you doesn't mean they *are* better than you. Remember: your spiritual DNA is perfect. Whatever makes those people successful or capable is within you, too.

We all share the same human experience, and you can always find points of resonance in other people's lives. Your current life may have nothing in common with Bill Gates's current life, but Bill Gates didn't become a success overnight. He faced rejection and struggles, just like you.

It's vital that you seek out those similarities in others to find the right models for you. Once I was able to identify all my connections with Oprah, I was better able to believe in my ability to achieve more. If you only look at a person's successes and the ways in which they're different from you, then of course it's easy to think that the similarities don't exist. Instead, start from the similarities and then begin modeling the thoughts and behaviors you wish to adopt.

Once you choose who you want to model yourself after, you have many different means of gaining the needed information. For me, this has meant becoming an avid reader. Whatever you want to learn about—grief, addiction, confidence, purpose, literally anything you can think of—there's a book about it. Reading books is a practical system to implement modeling. You can also listen to audiobooks, watch interviews, or YouTube videos of your models, read articles, or even get daily tweets of inspiration. With computers and smartphones, a world of information is at your fingertips.

We are brilliant, complex creatures that learn in a multitude of ways, so take in as much information as you can in as many ways as you can, and find what works for you. Keep in mind that what works for you today may not work for you tomorrow. Different mediums of information provide different experiences and trigger different moods and energies. The kind of energy that will best serve you may change. Some days reading a book may be what you need, while other days it's watching a YouTube video. The important thing is to immerse yourself in new ideas that align with who you want to become.

CHOOSING MODELS

Where you end up finding your models depends on who you are and who you desire to become. One way to find the right models is to search for people who have experienced similar adversity to you—people whose pain points resonate with your own.

If you want to figure out how to handle a specific adversity or a certain downloaded paradigm, it makes sense to gravitate toward those who have also experienced those things. If you're going through a divorce, you'll be attracted to the stories of people who have been divorced. If you grew up without a father or mother, you'll be attracted to those who also experienced a parent's absence.

Your models don't need to be identical copies of you, though. Even if they didn't experience your exact adversity, they likely experienced the same general feelings as you. We all struggle. We all feel rejected. We all feel like we're not good enough.

Right now, we're fighting for more representation of African Americans and other minorities in television and film. Television and cinema help develop our imagination, which controls our consciousness. Representation is vital. We need to see ourselves in the stories and images we see on our TV screens. Today, representation is increasing, but in the late '80s there were limited black characters, particularly black female characters, for me to model. Because of this reality, I connected with the heart of characters, and no one had heart like the "Italian Stallion" Rocky Balboa. It didn't matter that he wasn't black. He was an underdog, with one-in-a-million odds. He was a real-life hero to me. Rocky was a dreamer, but he also had flaws and imperfections. I saw myself in Rocky.

My favorite scene and quote from *Rocky I* is the night before his fight with Creed when he's talking to Adrian about his fears. Rocky says, "Nobody's ever gone the distance with Creed, and if I can go that distance and that bell rings and I'm still standin', I'm gonna know for the first time in my life, that I weren't just another bum from the neighborhood." I love that: "if I can go that distance and that bell rings and I'm still standin'..." Wow, it gives me chills when I read it. I could connect with that, and I watched the *Rocky* movies over and over again, especially *Rocky IV*, which is my favorite of the franchise.

As you peel back the layers of people, you will often find unexpected similarities. In my studies, I discovered that Steve Jobs, the creator of Apple computers and the iPhone, was adopted and struggled with obsessively seeking approval, just like me. This crazy obsession lived at the core of everything he created.

I found out that, like me, Colin Powell wasn't an amazing student—Colin Powell, the former four-star general and first African American appointed to the position of US Secretary of State, who currently has a building named after him at the same college where he struggled academically. In Powell's own words:

> I had a straight C average all the way through high school and the City College of New York—I'm not sure how I got

in...I got straight As in ROTC, so the administration rolled my As into the overall grade point average and that got me to a 2.0.[6]

I can't tell you how liberating it is to find yourself in someone else who has reached an unprecedented level of success despite adversity. Maybe Wake Forest University will name a building after me one day.

I've probably watched every episode of *Inside the Actors Studio* with James Lipton, and a countless number of the featured actors spoke of the rejection they'd experienced, the times they were told, "No," "No," "No." You unearth all these facts about people and discover that *they're just like you*. It's liberating to hear these truths because you realize that these people, who are just like you, have gone on to accomplish great things.

Because you'll always be able to find *some* similarities with others, another great way to find models is to start from the future. Who do you want to become? What traits do you want to have? Who in the world exhibits those desired traits?

In my case, I want to be happy, healthy, and wealthy. I want to be a servant leader. I want to be a strong, con-

---

6   Nikki Schwab, "Colin Powell: Bad Student," *Washington Examiner*, May 30, 2012, https://www.washingtonexaminer.com/colin-powell-bad-student.

fident woman and an empowering speaker. So, I study people who reflect those desired traits, abilities, and accomplishments. Your own models will naturally reflect you and your interests.

Consider building an imaginary board of advisers. Stock it with a good variety of models. If you want to work on financial goals, then include a few financially successful individuals, especially if you suffer from a mindset of lack due to growing up in poverty. If you struggle with codependency, then you'll want the support of strong women and should put a few on your board. If you want to be a surgeon, include successful, well-respected surgeons. If you want to be closer to God or stronger spiritually, find a spiritual adviser for your board. Then, whenever you want help in a chosen area, you plug into the source you've already chosen for guidance in that area. It is vitally important that you seek information from people that are qualified to help you achieve your next level of success.

Having a board of advisors is a system. I recommend actually writing down who is on your board. You want to be as organized as possible, with a plan before you get to adversity and discomfort. If you already have a plan of who to "consult," then you'll be more confident and courageous as you move forward.

FAMOUS, WELL-KNOWN MODELS

People are often afraid or lack the initiative to go outside their immediate circles for models. My earliest model was my first basketball coach, and he was a great influence on me, but if I hadn't also modeled people outside my immediate circle, I wouldn't have reached my full potential.

Most of the time great models won't drop into our laps, but one of the great things about the world today is how easily accessible information is. With the plethora of information available, you can model people you'll never meet or speak to. Well-known people can make great models because they have credibility and often share specific information about their journeys and struggles. You have such a great variety of models to choose from too, as I've personally discovered.

My Famous Models

Oprah has been my most influential model, but she's far from my *only* model. I've modeled many different individuals, both famous and not.

At an early age, I was obsessed with Michael Jordan, because he played basketball and was from North Carolina. Jordan is the best basketball player this world has ever known, and I was fortunate enough to have been born in 1980, so that I could witness firsthand his greatness. When his VHS tapes *Playground* and *Come Fly with Me* came out, I watched them religiously, and I wore number 23 because of him. I would watch Jordan play and then immediately go outside to practice, trying to mimic his fadeaway jumper.

Many of my models came from the art of hip-hop. Another advantage of being born in 1980 was witnessing in real time the genesis of America's most ambitious art form: hip-hop. Hip-hop artists were self-made, and I knew I would have to be self-made, too. For kids growing up in the '90s, hip-hop music and culture swept us off of our feet. It was ambitious, it was authentic, it was bold, it was cool, and it was raw. The music painted a picture of what was happening in black communities around the country, and young people loved it. It reflected a truth that wasn't being told anywhere else.

Jay-Z, Diddy, Will Smith, and Queen Latifah were particularly powerful models for me. The key behavior I learned from them was how to add layers to what I do and continue growing. Each of these artists constantly worked to present a newer and better version of themselves. They evolved as musicians, and they didn't stop at being rappers. They became producers, actors, and business executives who worked to use their platform to add more value to the world. By following their model, I too have challenged myself to become more than just a basketball coach. I've gone from player to assistant coach to head coach to public speaker, entrepreneur, and author.

At times, even music itself was a model for me. Both hip-hop music and gospel music expressed the themes of struggle, adversity, hopelessness, abuse, and oppression. Making adversity your advantage is the core message of both genres. The music made me feel less alone. It helped me to understand myself. It also empowered me and gave me hope. Gospel music especially taught me that healing is a feeling. Resilience is a feeling, and when this feeling is expressed through song, it can transform someone's life. In gospel music, this process is embraced with worship.

In a similar vein, I've looked to servant leaders as models for how to take injustices like slavery and lack of civil rights to spark indomitable energy for change. All my vision boards include photos of Martin Luther King, Malcolm X, and Gandhi. On my desk I keep a black-and-white photo of Emmett Till's mom and Martin Luther King signing the Voting Rights Act with FDR. These individuals inspire me to serve others and work toward the greater good. Their sacrifices opened doors and opportunities for others, and if they can do it, I can do it. We share the same human spirit. Their leadership and strength is part of my DNA.

I've also modeled myself after many self-improvement

thought leaders. Everything in this book came from somewhere. I didn't pull it out of thin air; I learned it from over a decade of studying people like Tony Robbins, Bob Proctor, Lisa Nichols, Don Miguel Ruiz, Stephen Covey, Eckhart Tolle, Wayne Dyer, George Pratt, Jim Rohn, Zig Ziglar, John Maxwell, Les Brown, and Napoleon Hill.

These people taught me how my brain works and how my feelings and thoughts combine to create my life. Modeling these people and the thoughts and behaviors they advocate allowed me to take control over my life and to connect with and understand people better.

Now that I'm running my own company, I've sought out leaders in the business world to model. Steve Jobs is one of those models. He was a visionary, able to see something bigger and greater outside of what was currently there. He showed me the power of the imagination, which is the single most powerful force we have to create change. I also looked to Howard Schultz, a former athlete and the founder of Starbucks, and Ted Turner, founder of TNT, TBS, and CNN, to discover ways to build my business dreams.

I have been especially interested in the early African American business leaders, the ones who did it against the odds, before anybody else thought it could be done—people like Bob and Sheila Johnson, creators of Black Entertainment Television (BET), and John Johnson, founder of *Ebony* and *Jet* magazines. These companies sought to portray black people in a new way: not as barbaric or threatening but as successful, smart, classy, and family centered. They gave voice to black people's true stories. They gave us some of our first images of African Americans from a black lens. I admire these founders for their courage and commitment to positive storytelling and positive imagery of African Americans.

Finally, I was completely obsessed with *Inside the Actors Studio* for a year and a half. I watched every single one. I love actors and artists. I love their failures and how they talk about them. They work in a field that is rife with rejection, and as a result, they are simultaneously so vulnerable while also being so confident, so sure of themselves. Anyone who performs, including athletes, has to deal with people judging them, criticizing them, and telling them they're not good enough, reminding them of what they could've done better. The actors and performers I've modeled myself after have taught me that, to find success, I have to swallow the negativity, get up, and try again.

With all of my models, I learned about their successes but paid even more attention to their failures and struggles and how they became successful.

EVERYDAY MODELS IN YOUR IMMEDIATE ENVIRONMENT

Not all models need to be famous, wildly successful people. I've spent a lot of time emphasizing how this is *your* journey and no one is going to help you but yourself. Ultimately, you are the only one who is responsible for your outcome. However, that doesn't mean you can't find help and support from people close to you. In fact, you can likely find positive role models in your immediate environment, whether it be a parent, a professor, a minister, a coach, a supervisor, or someone else important to you.

These role models can be incredibly powerful because you can actually interact with them. Instead of reading about how they handled something, you can see it with your own eyes. They can also give you firsthand experience of how to build a healthy relationship and communicate well. They may even become mentors for you.

My Everyday Models

When I was young, the McDowell family and Dana Conte were key models for me.

Heather McDowell was one of my best friends. One day, when I was eleven, her father, Mike, noticed me shooting on a side basket in our middle school gymnasium, and he asked me whether I'd like to play summer Amateur Athletic Union (AAU) basketball. I remember thinking, *Play more basketball? Be out of the house? Great!*

Over the years, the McDowells became family to me. In college, when I didn't want to go home over the breaks, I'd go to Mike and Marsha McDowells' house instead. I'd visit my mom during the day, and then I'd go back to the McDowells' to sleep at night. They gave me a home. They were my only example of a healthy home, a loving family with a mom and a dad who took care of their children. No lies, no verbal abuse, no physical abuse, no sexual abuse—just normal. Mike is the only father figure I've ever known, Marcia has always been my second mom, and I needed both of them. They were consistent in their love and care for me and made me feel like I mattered. Still today, nothing has changed. We are family.

It's thanks to Mike McDowell and his suggestion to play AAU basketball that I met Dana Conte. Dana was my first basketball coach, and he is still my mentor today. Because my mom always worked two or three jobs, she didn't have the time to drive me to practices and tournaments throughout the state. So Dana, in addition to Mike and Marsha, made sure I got where I needed to be. Then, at the end of my first AAU season, he told me, "If you ever want me to come pick you up and take you to the YMCA to shoot or work on your game, just give me a call. I go every day after work."

I took him up on his offer. For five years, when I wasn't in my high school season or my summer AAU season, I called him every day. And every day he came and picked me up. I didn't have a membership to the YMCA, but Dana had friends who worked the front desk and would either sneak me in, get me visitor passes to use, or pay for me to get in, if his friends weren't working.

Interestingly enough, my father went to the same YMCA that Dana would take me to. My dad was a fit military man, and he would be at the top of the track, running, while I was down on the basketball court working on my jump shot with a twenty-five-year-old white man. Sometimes my father would come down and say hey to me, and sometimes he wouldn't. The contrast between how these two men—my father and my coach—treated me was stark. Outside of my grandmother, Dana has been the most reliable person I've ever had in my life. He took an interest in me and honored his word.

I believe that God will send you "your people," who most times never appear how you would've imagined. The McDowells and Dana were "my people," sent to me through the law of attraction. Through my deep belief and love for basketball, I attracted the right people, places, and information I needed in order to become the person that I desired to be. Clearly defining your mission will save your life. They gave me opportunities to get out of my house and be in a safe place. They fed me and cared for me and gave me the attention I so desperately needed that I wasn't getting anywhere else. The statistics for sexually abused children are bleak: some studies estimate between 47 and 82 percent of women in jail were sexually abused as children,[7] and strong correlations have been found between childhood sexual abuse and obesity in later life. Many people are not fortunate enough to recover from the trauma of that hurt. The McDowells and Dana were my life raft, and I am a better person now because I had their example to follow. Who are "your people?"

YOUR PAST SELF AS MODEL

I recommend using your past self as a model as well. Think about points in your life when you overcame something. Reflect on your past experiences when you turned adversity into an advantage. Then model your previous success.

For instance, if you're currently facing a major transition, you can look back at the previous transition times

---

7   Chandra Bozelko, "Sexual Abuse Survivors Deserve Help, Not Punishment," *Huffpost*, February 18, 2018, https://www.huffingtonpost.com/entry/opinion-bozelko-sexual-abuse-prison_us_5a871e17e4b00bc49f43c39a.

of your life, like the transition from middle school to high school. You likely felt nervous at first, but by the time you graduated, you felt more confident and comfortable. You can take that experience and apply it to your current transition. Reflect on a time you were laid off from your job, went through a divorce, or faced some other challenge and didn't know how you would make it. We all have made it through some difficult times. Think of a few specific actions you took that helped you move forward, and mirror those. Before too long, you'll be feeling more confident.

Oftentimes, when I'm discouraged, I have to look in the rearview mirror and say, "Man, you know, you grew up with over fifty foster kids in and out of your home. You were sexually abused at eight years old, and your mother told you that you weren't pretty or very smart. You watched a friend get shot and killed. Then you lost your best friend in the same year. You were never supposed to get out of that county. But you ended up being able to live out your dreams."

Reflecting on the past adversities you've survived will assure you that you are a strong individual and will figure out your current situation, too. We all feel weak at times, but there's also a layer of strength in us that can move mountains. We just have to remind ourselves that it's there.

MODELING THOUGHTS

The first step to modeling another person's thoughts is to study their life. Jim Rohn said, "The reason people don't succeed is that they don't expose themselves to pre-existing information." Whatever you're trying to become, you have access to information about it. Technology, finance, athletics, theater, arts, music—there are infinite possibilities when you understand that you have infinite potential. Anything you can think of, the information is there for you to get one step closer. It's your responsibility to take ownership and go seek out the information you need.

Seek to answer these questions about your chosen models:

- How did they deal with their pain?
- How did they identify their gifts?
- Who helped them?
- What kind of decisions did they have to make to move forward?
- What were their failures?
- What books did they read, or what resources did they utilize?

Then, based on what you learn, borrow information and apply it to your own life. For example, Oprah dealt with her pain by focusing on her gift of intelligence and seeking to do well in school. I borrowed that idea and began focusing my thoughts on my goals instead of on my adversity.

As with everything in this book, modeling must be repetitive. You must continue studying your models, as different pieces of information will jump out at you at different points in your journey. I've "graduated" from studying certain people, found new people to study, and stuck with other people for years and years. I've been studying Oprah Winfrey for fifteen years. If I had only studied her for two years and then stopped, I'm not sure I would be writing this book today. I've learned vastly different things from her over the years based on the points at which I encountered her in my own journey.

Wherever you are in your journey, by learning about your models you will begin to change your thoughts in two key ways. First, you will believe in yourself more. Second, you will become more heroic.

BELIEVE IN YOURSELF

Models provide evidence. This is why they are so important. We need to know that people who are just like us have gotten through adversity. We need evidence to build our faith in our own future success. Anytime we can increase our awareness and knowledge of something, we become less afraid of it.

As you study your models, you'll realize that all your heroes, all the people you look up to, experienced fear. They procrastinated. They had trouble losing weight. They cheated on their husband or wife. They had money issues. They drank too much. They were insecure. They made mistakes. They struggled. They didn't make perfect grades. They were fired.

In uncovering these truths, you realize that we all struggle in similar ways and that we all make mistakes. For me, it was liberating to hear that successful people had also fallen flat on their faces and made poor decisions in the past. Knowing that others had done the same things I had, allowed me to forgive myself, to release myself to move on.

The thing that distinguishes us is not our adversities or our mistakes but how we respond to setbacks—whether or not we get back up after being knocked down. That is an empowering realization: your adversity isn't holding you back; you're holding yourself back. You can't change your adversity, but you can change yourself. This is why the needed power is in your hands.

Models give us the faith that we too can become successful. If they were able to fight through all of their challenges, then we can too. If Oprah could go from being a poor, sexually abused girl in backwoods Mississippi to a billionaire tycoon, I can at least write a book. I can at least try to impact some kids' lives and touch my community. I can at least do *something*.

Seeing what others have accomplished will expand and enlarge your vision of what's possible for you.

BE HEROIC

When you study your models, you will see that they struggled. You will see that their mom left them or they went through a divorce or they suffered with a drug addiction. You'll see that something knocked them down.

Then you'll also see that they got up. You'll see that they activated their faith and strength. You'll see that they called upon the hero in them. And you'll recognize that you will have to do the same from time to time. You're going to have to put your cape on. That's the deal.

You don't have to be a hero every day. Life won't require it from you every day, but it will require it from you eventually. That's why the daily practice of building your mental muscles, understanding who you are and who you want to be, and eliminating all the things that don't add value to your life are so important. When you do come to the fork in the road—the cancer diagnosis, the job loss, the death— you can attack your adversity in a different way. It may knock you down briefly, but it's not going to knock you out, because you've built up the needed muscle. You'll be able to put on your cape and say, "Not today."

Be prepared to be active in your own rescue. Tomorrow the bottom could fall out for me. My company could collapse. I could not make another dime. But I'm equipped mentally to be okay because I understand who I am. I've been through fires before, and I've walked out of them, so I'll be okay no matter what happens tomorrow.

You should be prepared to use your strengths and gifts for others, too. Part of being your best self is supporting others when they need help. We're all connected, and we should help each other in our journeys when we can. You never know when you're going to look up and realize that you can use your strengths and gifts to be a model for someone else. Maybe you'll become the Dana Conte or Mike and Marsha McDowell in someone's life. You could be someone's anchor for weeks, months, or even years—however long it takes for them to see the beauty in their journey and become their own hero.

I was in a leadership position on a college campus for fourteen years, and there were times that I had to step up and be the hero for my players when they weren't in a place where they could do it for themselves yet. I had to be the person to tell a kid that her dad was passing away and she needed to go home. I had to be there for a player who was gang-raped by five football players. I believe that sometimes our stories aren't always for us. Sometimes we go through things so that we can help others, and in my case, my experiences uniquely equipped me to provide my players the support they needed.

I encourage you to model what has been modeled for you. Be the hero—in your own story and in others' stories.

MODELING BEHAVIOR

Later on, in Chapter 6, I will talk about identifying and stating your cause. Once you determine your cause, modeling takes on a new layer of meaning. You can see the steps your models took to reach their goals, and you can mimic them. This transforms your cause from an amorphous, abstract concept to something concrete and real, something you can work on every day.

As you look for behavior to model, focus on doing the things you're good at, doing the things you don't like to do, and doing the next thing.

DO THE THINGS YOU'RE GOOD AT

As I'll discuss further in Chapter 6, it's key that you identify the things you're good at. Your purpose will be aligned with your unique talents and gifts, so go deep with the things you're good at. This will allow you to discover your purpose, which will be your anchor when you face storms of adversity. It will give you something that is greater than your pain, something into which you can funnel the energy of your pain.

In order to fully develop your unique talents, you should seek out models who have mastered similar skills. You can learn from them how to refine your gifts and become not just good or great but extraordinary.

I identified at an early age that I was good at basketball, and for many years, I focused my energy in that direction. Like most people, though, I'm good at several different things, and as I've grown, my purpose has shifted. In my role as a coach, I realized that, for as good as I've been at basketball, my true gift is in my ability to inspire people to enlarge their vision of what's possible. Over time, I funneled my energy into this purpose, and now that's what I'm doing for a living. I'm standing up on stages, communicating to people how great they are and showing them how to make adversity work to their advantage.

DO THE THINGS YOU DON'T LIKE TO DO

As I've mentioned previously, change is scary. Some of the new thoughts and behaviors you seek to model are going to feel uncomfortable. Your old paradigm will want to step in and tell you to go back to what you used to do.

Your goals and your dreams, not your old thoughts and behaviors, have to run the show. Your new story must control all of your decisions. That means, initially, you may have to do things you don't like to do. This is necessary to replace toxic behavior with healthy behavior. Eventually the new behavior will become habitual, and it will no longer feel uncomfortable. Think about it like going to the gym. At first, it's hard to get the motivation to go to the gym, but if you stick with it, the practice eventually becomes a habit. Then, it's not only easier to go, but you actually *enjoy* going.

Remember: repetition, repetition, repetition! That's how you train your subconscious. If you only eat right once every seven days, then you're not going to create habitual behaviors that lead to results. It's no different than anything we're trying to accomplish in our lives. You want to learn how to play the piano? It's the same thing. You're going to get there faster if you do it five out of seven days a week, as opposed to two out of seven days.

You can use the power and depth of the adversity you've experienced for motivation. Your adversity can be the force that makes you wake up and write in your gratitude journal or read your affirmations aloud. Your adversity can be the catalyst for change. It can be the impetus that convinces you to get out of that bad relationship or to quit the job you hate. The energy of your adversity can be the trigger that makes you do those things you don't initially want to do.

DO THE NEXT THING

Don't try to do everything all at once. Focus on doing just the next thing. Work on adopting just a few key thoughts and behaviors at a time. This is not an "I want abs tomorrow" type of deal. You're not going to get abs in a day, and you're not going to make adversity your advantage in a day. Just start where you are, with what you've got, and go from there. Don't worry about perfection, because it doesn't exist, and don't worry about failure. Don't worry about anything except taking the next best action that you know how to take.

The speed of implementation is more important than the quantity of things implemented. When I first started studying Oprah, I didn't try to model a hundred different things Oprah did. If I'd done that, I would have been overwhelmed, and I wouldn't have actually implemented anything. Instead, I started with just a couple of the things that made sense for where I was in my journey at the time. Then, after mastering those things and growing, I was able to implement more strategies, and then some more, and then some more, until I was experiencing exponential growth.

In just three years—thirty-six months—your life can change completely. Whether it's the way you feel about yourself, how happy you are, your weight, your job, or whatever you want to change, you can make drastic leaps, but only if you go into application mode.

Remember: you're never going to feel ready. Your subconscious is going to try to rationalize and convince you to stick with your old, comfortable habits. Don't let it. You already know that your old ways of being are not going to give you the results you want. If you want new results, you have to do new things, and you have to act *now*. Always keep looking forward. The most important step will always be the next one.

MODELING ENVIRONMENT

I believe environment is the number one indicator of who we become. You can tell a lot about a person from their environment—their job, the food they eat, their home, their car, the people they hang out with. Do they cook meals, or do they eat fast food? Do they have $100,000 or more in their savings account, or do they not have a savings account at all? Do they have strong spiritual beliefs? Do they value family and quality relationships?

It is vital that you create an environment that nurtures your gifts and talents. I did this growing up by covering my bedroom walls with Michael Jordan posters and displaying all my trophies. I wasn't aware of what I was doing at the time, but I was creating a space that nurtured and protected my dreams.

Environment can be transformative, and you can model environment just like you model thoughts and behaviors. Identify the types of environments that have led to success for others, and work to implement such a space in your own life. While we may not always be able to move someplace entirely new, we *can* control our environments by choosing where we focus our attention and who we spend time with. And remember: your imagination allows you to go anywhere you want. When you visualize yourself fulfilling your deepest wishes, you trigger an empowering feeling. If you live in that feeling of your wishes fulfilled, your subconscious will accept your dreams as reality.

WHERE DO YOU FOCUS YOUR ATTENTION?

Where do you spend your time and energy? A dead-end job? Toxic relationships? An addiction?

Okay, now where do you *want* to be focusing your time and energy? What pursuits or situations would contribute to your growth? Create a checklist for what you want in your environment.

For me, I wanted an environment where I could help more people and leave a ripple effect of positivity long after I'm gone. I wanted an environment of love and growth, where I could be in complete control of my life and work. I loved being a coach, but when I was honest with myself, it was an environment that I had outgrown. I felt I was putting my effort into something that was no longer adding value to my spirit, so I resigned. And I built an environment based on who I wanted to become—an environment where I could practice becoming a speaker, where I could be my own boss, write books, and focus on economic wealth while also having time, freedom, and the opportunity to inspire people to dream big.

You don't necessarily need to quit your job or upend your life; even small changes in your environment can have big ramifications. For example, back when I was drinking heavily, my environment revolved around alcohol. I spent my time at bars and social events, always looking for a reason to celebrate, expecting to be drunk. That environment assisted in my excessive alcohol consumption, which, as I already stated, nearly derailed my life. Now I don't go to bars to get drunk. I don't hang around people who drink to get drunk. I don't drink socially. I don't keep alcohol in my house. I'll never get another DUI because

I've removed alcohol from my environment. Good or bad, positive or negative, it's hard for something to become a reality if it's not in your environment.

If your environment is aligned with your goals, you will achieve them more easily. Design your environment so that you are spending your time on worthwhile pursuits. Remove distractions and temptations and surround yourself with positive influences. Make everything intentional.

WHO DO YOU SPEND YOUR TIME WITH?

Who you choose to spend your time with is *key*. You will naturally model the behavior of those around you, so you must choose those people wisely. Something you'll likely notice when you study your models is that successful people only hang around people who match their energy. You must become a master at owning your space, and you must only invite people into your world who deserve your energy and who can add value to your space.

When it comes to the people in my life, I live by two acronyms: OQP and PPP.

OQP stands for "only quality people." Period. That's a nonnegotiable. I don't do negativity. I don't do bad energy. I don't do pity parties. That doesn't mean I completely avoid people like that; they just don't get to live permanently in my world. Only people whose thinking and ideals align with mine become a significant part of my life.

PPP stands for "productive, profitable, or positive." Think of the five people you spend the most time with. Are they positive? If so, great. If not, they'd better be making you money. If they're not making you money, they'd better be helping you be productive. PPP is a good way to figure out if your inner circle is helping you reach your desired outcomes and to weed out people who aren't contributing to your life.

Cutting people out of your life can be painful and difficult, but you must put yourself and your growth first. Sometimes other people simply aren't at a stage in their own journey that aligns with yours. You must continue on your own path while letting them follow theirs. This will open up room in your life for the right people to enter.

ELEMENTS OF ENVIRONMENT YOU CAN'T CONTROL

What about elements of your environment that you can't control? I believe that you can do whatever you make up your mind to do, and you likely control far more aspects of your environment than you realize.

Many times when people say they "can't" avoid someone

in their life, it's because they feel an obligation to that person. Often it may be a family member or a significant other.

At twenty-three I decided that my mother wasn't adding value to my life and so she could not be a part of my world. I was incredibly cutthroat in that way. I don't recommend this for everyone. As I've discussed, I don't have strong ties to family, and that has been a blessing in a way. I feel no obligation to have anybody in my world who doesn't deserve to be there, even if they are "family." I've never felt so strongly attached to another being that I need them in my space even though they cause me discomfort or pain or take away my joy.

Many people, though, have to face the internal conflict of recognizing someone is a negative influence but still loving that person and feeling an obligation to them. Sometimes it's necessary to sit down with that person and have an adult conversation. Consider letting the person in question know that you're trying to do x, y, and z and can't afford to dedicate your time and energy to the relationship. "My goal is to finish my master's degree while raising my child" or "My goal is to become the best version of myself. In order to do that I must direct my focus and attention elsewhere."

Sometimes you will have to make decisions that are in

your best interest and not worry about the opinions of others. That can be really tough, but it will be better for you in the long run. Your ability to establish boundaries for people will aid you tremendously in making adversity your advantage.

If for some reason you can't completely cut someone out of your life—for example, maybe you have to interact with your ex because of children you have together—set clear boundaries. Refuse to give any more time or energy to that individual than necessary.

Also give yourself permission to change your mind. That's what I had to do leaving my coaching career. I loved basketball more than anything. I identified as a basketball coach, and if you'd asked me ten years ago, I would've said I was going do it for the rest of my life. But I changed my mind, and that's okay. I grew. I evolved. I became more conscious of who I am and what I wanted. If you are challenging yourself to grow, things will change. You have the right to change your mind in regard to your relationships, your job, your life—everything.

If you do find yourself in an environment you can't improve, the first thing you must do is decide that this space you're in and the people you are around are temporary. Begin planning ahead for a way out. If you're emotionally or financially dependent on someone, strategize a way to become independent. It's liberating to be free from worry about someone else's opinions, approval, financial assistance, or emotional support. You can be handicapped by reliance on these things. Independence will give you the freedom to be more of yourself.

Next, after deciding that the situation is temporary, begin living out of your imagination. Create a new story for the situation. When we speak negatively about negative people and negative situations, we only bring more negativity to our journeys. If you instead adopt a positive attitude, the law of attraction will work to bring more positivity into your life. Remember: the subconscious accepts everything you feed it.

Maybe your boss doesn't value you and puts you down, but you can't afford to quit your job before finding a new one. First, decide the situation is temporary, and start looking for a new job with a more productive, positive environment. At the same time, pledge to see the best in your boss and decide that he'll see the best in you, too. Communicate that aloud to yourself every day so that you can see him through a better lens. Look for the lessons this moment is supposed to teach you, and work to be grateful for them.

MODEL OTHERS

Success is a process. Jay-Z didn't get signed to a major record label right away. No, he sold CDs out of his car. Beyoncé wasn't a Grammy winner right away, though she's now the most nominated woman in the award's history. Michael Jackson was told he couldn't transition from bubblegum pop music with the Jackson 5 to be a serious solo artist. Similarly, you're not going to achieve all that you want right away. Luckily, successful people leave behind blueprints for you to follow.

Seeing how others made the journey will reveal the steps you can take to get there, too. You don't need to reinvent the wheel. Take advantage of all the information and wisdom your models provide. Find the right thoughts, behaviors, and environments to model. Then be a model for someone else.

TAKE YOUR DAILY G AND E VITAMINS

We are hardwired for forward movement and progress. From the moment we are born, we begin growing. First smile, first step, first word. Then we go to school and continue learning every single day. Eventually, we get out into the "real world," and we begin to stagnate. We reach a certain age and think that we've made it. We are who we are, and that's it. We stop learning. We stop cultivating our skills and improving our attitude. We stop being curious. We stop using our imagination. We stop thinking.

However, the moment you stop growing, you are no longer really living. Anything not growing is dead. Even though we were birthed for growth, most people fall into complacency. In order to help sustain your growth and stick with the refuse-to-lose process, you should practice gratitude and empathy—these are your G and E vitamins. Gratitude and empathy are 100 percent within your control, and if you can lock in and focus on these states of mind, they can be transformative.

It's important that you take these vitamins *daily*. If you stop exercising, you will lose the muscle mass you gained, and if you don't regularly practice gratitude and empathy, you will begin to lose the energy needed to sustain your growth. The refuse-to-lose mindset is not a one-and-done permanent fix for all your problems. It is a way of life.

Practicing gratitude and empathy will change the way you see people and the world, creating a heart of forgiveness and compassion.

MY LESSON IN GRATITUDE AND EMPATHY

In November 2011, I got a call that my mom was sick in the hospital. I didn't fully understand the gravity of the situation yet, but I knew my mother wasn't in the best health and didn't take care of herself as well as she should. When I went to see her, the doctors explained that she had been living with untreated pneumonia for months. They would have to perform a surgery on her lungs, and they didn't think she would survive the procedure.

I had spent all of my twenties hating my mother. I'd judged her and blamed her for my pain. I'd judged her for getting married so many times, for not putting me first in her decisions, for taking in so many foster kids, for not being the mother I wanted and needed, for not being *better*.

In a way, because I didn't have a healthy, loving family, I made basketball my family instead. It was always basketball this and basketball that. Basketball had gotten me out of my toxic home environment. Basketball had given me mentors. Basketball had given me a full scholarship to my dream school. Basketball had helped me purchase my first home. Basketball had given me acceptance and love. Basketball, in essence, had saved my life.

I thought I was fine with basketball being the center of my life, with my mother pushed to the sidelines, but when the doctors told me she might not even make it to see the next week, I was terrified. I suddenly realized that she meant a lot more to me than I was letting on. My anger had been generated through extreme sadness and brokenness. I didn't want her to die, and I definitely didn't want her to die with our relationship fractured.

My mother had written me a letter earlier that year, telling me how my behavior was hurting her and how she wanted our relationship to be better. I'd previously ignored the letter, as I had made an intentional decision to keep her out of my life so that I could move on. I knew, though, that I would never be completely free of the anger I felt toward her until I forgave her, and I also knew that if she died with everything between us still broken, I would regret it. I couldn't afford to live with anger and regret forever. For her sake as well as my own, I had to at least try to repair our relationship.

I made a vow, praying out loud to God, "For as long as you allow her to live, I will honor her. I'll be the best daughter I possibly can be. She will come first. Nothing will come before her—not basketball, not my job, not my players, not anybody in my community. She will be priority number one. Just give me time to do right by her."

She pulled through to the next week and then lived for two and a half more years. For that period of time, I kept my word to God. I didn't know how long she would live, but I committed to loving her completely every single day. I'm grateful that I'd reached a place in my personal development where I was able to do this.

My brother was living on the other side of the country by this time, so my mother's care fell to me. I coordinated everything for her because she didn't have anybody else to do it for her. I lived almost four hours away, but I still made it to her doctor's appointments and visited her regularly. I'd drive seven to eight hours in a day just to sit with her for a couple of hours. Throughout this time, I continued to work as a head coach, first at Tusculum and then at UNC Wilmington, where I began working in May 2012.

In those two and a half years, I watched her deteriorate from the strong, formidable woman who had always brought the hammer down in our home to a small, fragile husk weighing less than a hundred pounds. The entire experience was incredibly difficult but also incredibly healing. We were able to have needed conversations, create new memories, and achieve a peace in our relationship.

Sitting at the foot of her bed in the hospital and nursing home, I was able to forgive and even appreciate her. When I was a baby, she *chose* me. I could have ended up in the foster-care system, but instead I had a home. It may not have been perfect, but it was my home. When I flipped the light switch, lights came on. When I twisted the sink's knobs, water came out. It was my mother who had given me that, and I'd never given her the credit she deserved for choosing me and providing for me. For the first time in as long as I could remember, I finally felt more love and gratitude than anger when it came to my mother.

My anger dissipated further as I realized and accepted

that she had been doing the best she could. A key component of empathy is understanding that everyone in our lives is doing the best they can. We might think their best isn't good enough, and we are entitled to our opinion, but it's still their best. If they could give us more, they would. My mother gave me everything she could, and you know what? For as much as I had blamed her and bemoaned my circumstances, she must've done something right, because any success that I've had is a reflection of her efforts.

The gratitude and empathy muscles I cultivated by caring for my mother have allowed me to experience her, others, and the world in a different way. My G and E vitamins center me when I need to be centered. They raise my consciousness, giving me the emotional intelligence to deal with and manage intense emotions arising from loved ones' deaths, past sexual abuse, relationship problems, workplace issues, and disappointments triggered by past experiences. They have played pivotal roles in my growth and development, and they've been integral in making adversity my advantage.

GRATITUDE

Gratitude is an energy force that attracts more positive things to you. When you practice gratitude, your heart is full of a deep appreciation for something. When you awaken this energy source, you see the world through a more positive and grateful lens and thus attract more of what you appreciate.

The law of polarity says there's an opposite to everything. In and out, up and down, hot and cold, happy and sad, joy and pain, negative and positive, but never at the same time. A negative and a positive can't live in the same space, and as such, when you practice gratitude, it is very difficult to be an angry, pessimistic, negative individual.

Another law—the law of vibration—states that everything in the universe is vibrating; nothing rests. A rock may appear to be completely stationary, but if you look at it under a powerful microscope, you will see that the rock's component atoms are in fact vibrating. Vibration is energy, and so everything is energy.

Humans are not exempt from the law of vibration. At any given moment, you are vibrating at a certain frequency, and whatever vibrational frequency you put out into the universe is the energy you will attract back. By default, we vibrate at the frequency of our paradigms and belief systems, but often that frequency is not aligned with the version of ourselves we wish to become. Our vibrational frequency is a part of our subconscious mind, and we must learn to manifest results based on this fact. Gratitude is your secret weapon to maintaining the positive vibration you need to make the changes and get the results you desire. When you practice gratitude, you raise the frequency of your vibration, which will allow you to attract more things to be grateful for.

When we are faced with trauma and deep pain, like when we are grieving the death of a family member or friend or struggling with rejection, depression and sadness can set in. I have found gratitude to be the magical formula to counteract that. By choosing to change the focus of your thoughts, you can go from being sad to feeling deep appreciation.

The power of deep appreciation is apparent in the lives of all the successful people I have studied. The greatest among us all make use of gratitude as a key source of energy in their lives. Mastering this ability is vital to making adversity your advantage.

When you elevate your state of being to a certain vibration and frequency, you attract great things to your life. That's the dial on the radio station that you want. You're never going to get country music on the gospel station; you've got to find the frequency and get to the right channel. Fostering a state of gratitude is how you get the channel you want to be on.

Gratitude releases you. It has a profound effect on the way you think and feel, and thoughts and feelings become actions. At any given moment, I can think of my greatest gift—my grandmother, who loved me first and made me feel valued in this world—and with just that one thought, I can transform my entire state and see the world from a totally different lens. We all have that power.

You always have *something* to be grateful for. One of my favorite things that Oprah has said is that when you can't think of anything else to say thank you for, go to your last breath. Be grateful that you had an opportunity to breathe—to have oxygen and to be alive. Not everyone got that option.

Zig Ziglar, one of the first pioneers of personal development, said that the healthiest human emotion is gratitude. He emphasized the law of the universe that a negative thought cannot exist in the same space as a positive one. Many times, people don't *want* to be negative individuals, but due to their inherited belief systems, emotions, or paradigms, they can't control their triggers or thoughts. Gratitude is the key here. You might not be able to prevent the negative thoughts from occurring, but you can balance them by focusing on positive thoughts instead.

The architect R. Buckminster Fuller said, "Never change

things by fighting the existing reality...To change something, build a new model that makes the old model obsolete." You don't need to fight the negative thoughts. Simply embrace them and then choose another thought. In this way you build a new model—you rewrite your story.

It's hard to live a life of misery when you intentionally seek out gratitude. I advocate waking up every day and performing a practice of gratitude, acknowledging everything in your life that you appreciate. After you master a daily practice of appreciation, seek to have a continual attitude of gratitude. Walk through life looking for things to be grateful for—a sunny day, the checkout clerk who greets you with a smile, green lights on your way to work, a parking space right in front. You can find gratitude in all things.

GRATITUDE FOR YOUR PAIN

Often gratitude is about flipping your perspective. Sometimes that means focusing on the good in your life instead of the bad, and sometimes that even means being grateful for your pain.

When I struggle with gratitude, I always go back to my grandmother, because I loved her more than I have loved anything. I first knew what love is because of the way she looked at me and because of the energy she exuded when I came around. Her death was the most painful thing I've ever gone through. But I learned to give it a new meaning. I flipped my perspective of her death, telling myself, "Wow, I got to feel and experience her love. There's only one of her, and there's only one of me, and we had a unique relationship that was just ours." I'm grateful for that.

Nothing in your life is random or coincidental. Everything is happening perfectly as designed for you. If any single part of your life were different, then you would not be who you are today. If you hadn't done "this," then "that" wouldn't have happened.

When you are in the midst of your pain, it is difficult to see its purpose, but eventually, months or years down the line, you will be able to look back on your life and see how everything, the good and bad, has been leading you to your new point. The boyfriend who broke your heart prepared you to meet a new person who is a much better fit for you. The job you lost led you down a path that ended up advancing your career. The sexual abuse you suffered gave you the strength to help others in similar situations.

Working on self-awareness and asking yourself empowering questions can help you create a state of gratitude for your pain even before you can see the end result—the sun after the rain. When faced with difficulties, ask yourself, "What is this here to teach me? What do I need to learn from this experience? How can I use this to my advantage?" Then reassure yourself, "Whatever it is, I am ready to learn and evolve into the next version of me." When you look at pain and life through that lens, there's no way to be miserable. When you assign a new, powerful meaning to your past circumstances, pain, and adversity, you are no longer at the mercy of those negative emotions. You are in control.

Now when I look back at painful experiences, I am able to say, "I'm grateful that it happened that way." I'm grateful that I was raised in the home I was raised in and got introduced to basketball when I did, because it was my safety net. Later, I was able to make over a million dollars from coaching basketball, which I never intended to do. Now I'm in this position where I'm writing this book and telling this story. If any piece of my life had been different—if I hadn't been adopted, if I hadn't been sexually abused, if I hadn't felt depressed and worthless, if I hadn't turned to alcohol, if I hadn't lost close friends and family—I wouldn't have had the opportunity to become the person I am today or the person I dream to be in the future. I'm grateful for the life I have, and I'm grateful for my experiences.

People who have gone through a great deal of adversity always say, "Look how far I've come." The person from a third-world country who earns a degree from Harvard says, "Look how far I've come. I grew up on dirt floors, and here I am." The once angry, broken little black girl who becomes a leader and empowers young black women all over the world says, "Look how far I've come." The how-far-I've-come story is a powerful energy force. Gratitude for your humble beginnings can create energy that allows adversity to become a huge advantage. I always look in the rearview mirror and say, "God, look how far— look how far I've come."

Just as you can—and should—be grateful for past events, you can practice gratitude into the future, using your imagination to be grateful for things you don't have yet. As I wrote this book, I would look forward into the future and say, "I'm grateful that there's a great book called *Refuse to Lose: Seven Steps to Make Adversity Your Advantage*. It's an incredible book, and it's going to uplift so many people and add value to the world."

Using gratitude in this way helps create a future world that you want, like a self-fulfilling prophecy, the feeling of a wish fulfilled. You're downloading new information into your subconscious mind, and you are tuning yourself to the right vibration that will bring about the future. Gratitude gives you the energy you'll need to make your goals and dreams a reality.

GRATITUDE EXERCISES

To build an attitude of gratitude, start with concrete gratitude exercises.

One of the easiest and most effective internal gratitude exercises is to list what you're grateful for. Right now, go put pen to paper and write down ten things you are grateful for. That list is your starting point.

You should practice gratitude every single day. I recommend trying to start and end your day with gratitude. Personally, I write in a gratitude journal at night and read a gratitude list aloud each morning. There are also apps you can use to work on gratitude, like Five Minute Journal, Grateful, or My Gratitude Journal. Some apps give you an easy place to journal, and others send you reminders throughout the day to be grateful.

A gratitude journal is where you list the things that happened that day or in your life that you're grateful for. It can be as simple as being grateful for someone who held the door open for you. Oprah recommends keeping a gratitude journal because it makes you actively look for gratitude opportunities throughout your day. Wherever your attention goes, energy flows, so when you look for things to be grateful for, you cultivate an attitude of gratitude.

A gratitude list is just that—a list of the things you're

grateful for. This list can include past gratitudes (things that have already occurred) or future gratitudes (things that are still yet to come). You might come up with new items each day, repeat items, delete items, or add items. As your life changes, it makes sense that you will have new things to be grateful for, necessitating changes in your list. I've included an example gratitude list at the end of the book in case you need help getting started.

My personal daily gratitude list contains dozens of items, with both past and future gratitudes. I like to call out people's names in my gratitude list. By expressing my gratitude for them, I connect with their energy and their spirit, and maybe I can change the way I look at that person in the future. Sometimes I focus my gratitude on people I'm going to interact with that day. So I might say, "I'm so grateful for Kelsey. We're going to have a meeting today, and I know it's going to be incredible." Then, when it's time for the meeting, I enter from a place of appreciation and joy, and that person is going to feel the energy I've already begun building, helping ensure that the meeting is in fact incredible.

Other times, I express gratitude for the people who aren't in my day-to-day life anymore. This helps me feel connected to them despite distance or their absence. As an example, my brother lives in California, but I wake up every morning and say, "I'm grateful for Jamel, because he's the first friend I had. He introduced me to basketball and never begrudged me tagging along with him. He actually wanted me there, and his acceptance was the best gift. He was the first person to make me feel that I was good enough, and as an eight-year-old girl, his approval made me feel ten feet tall. He has irrefutably enhanced my life."

I do sometimes adjust my list, but for the most part, the core of my list remains the same. I like repeating the same items day after day because of the power in repetition. By ingraining your gratitude list into your subconscious mind, it can become one of the tools you use to help rewrite your story, reinforcing the thoughts you want to embody. For instance, each morning, I tell myself, "Today, when I walk out my door, if adversity comes my way, I know I'm a warrior. I am grateful that I'm capable of whatever I need to do or become, in order to get through and over whatever challenges arise."

First you decide, *This is who I want to be. This is what I'm about*. Then you can use your gratitude list to create that feeling of absolute certainty and faith in your wish fulfilled. Let's say you want to lose fifty pounds. Oftentimes, we speak so negatively about our bodies—our weight, our teeth, our hair, everything. We kill ourselves with self-criticism. The universe hears that, and we invite that energy back into our world.

Instead, rewrite the story of "I'm fat—I hate my body and need to lose weight" to "I am so grateful that I have this body. I am grateful that I have the physical health needed to get on the treadmill today. I'm grateful that I have access to good, nutritious food. Every day, I am getting healthier and healthier. I love my body." When you rewrite the story, you begin aligning to the energy frequency that is needed to bring about this future state. In this way, your gratitude will help you achieve the results you seek. Find things to love about yourself and be grateful for them, including the things you're working on daily.

In addition to creating an internal gratitude list, another effective practice is to express your gratitude for others. You can write a letter or sit down and have a conversation with the influential people in your life where you tell them that you appreciate them and value what they've given you. This is an activity I implemented during my coaching career. I always encouraged my players to write a letter to their parents or whoever had influenced them—that coach or teacher.

In all of these gratitude practices, it is imperative that you *believe your gratitude messages are true*, whether they're in the past, the present, or the future. At a Steve Harvey conference that I attended, he said that when he lists out what he's thankful for in his life and what he would like to appear in his life, he always ends his prayer with "I believe these things to be true, and I expect your abundance in my life and receive these things now." Words are powerful, but they need to be backed up by belief. You must *expect* your dreams and be open to receiving them. You can't just go through the motions here; you must *feel* it.

This goes back to the law of attraction. When you truly believe in what you are saying, you are setting the stage for those things to come true in reality. For example, if you tell yourself that you're grateful for the great attitude your son will demonstrate today and how he's going to be a better role model for his younger sister, you will be bringing a positive attitude and energy to the situation, allowing it to happen more readily in reality.

Any sort of gratitude practice, whether you express it internally or externally, is empowering. It changes the way you see the world and makes it hard to be miserable. Be authentic to yourself. Try out a variety of gratitude exercises and then do what works for *you*.

Gratitude gives you energy, and, unlike other sources of energy, this one is a renewable resource. If you feel like you don't have the energy to do whatever you're trying to do, go to gratitude. It will be your energizer, the battery in your back or your secret weapon.

EMPATHY

Gratitude is largely about what you give yourself. It's about adopting a more positive, appreciative mindset that will attract good things back to yourself. Empathy, on the other hand, is what you give to other people. Empathy is how you become a better person for others, for the outside world.

Empathy means you can understand someone else's thoughts, feelings, and experiences without experiencing it directly yourself and even without that person explicitly explaining it to you. Empathy is putting yourself in someone else's shoes and imagining how they must feel. If I am empathetic toward you, I can hear you. I'm sensitive to your struggles. I acknowledge you, your pain, and your efforts. Even though we haven't gone through the same experiences, I can see myself in you and understand your journey.

I learned the true meaning of empathy while watching my mother die for two and a half years. Watching someone's life come to an end will change the way you live your own life. I thought I was an empathetic person before my mother's illness, but I wasn't. I judged people that didn't behave the way I did or that had different beliefs than I did or that didn't share my thoughts and ideas. Doing this was wrong, and I was wrong for judging my mother the way I did all those years. I let my pain and anger stand in the way of my ability to see the human being in her and, more importantly, to see myself in her.

All of us can be empathetic, but many people practice empathy *selectively*. Society has separated us into boxes based on race, religion, gender, age, political beliefs, and dozens of other divisions. We're separated and encouraged to empathize only with our group. Our country was built on that energy, and that's why there's oppression and inequality. We disregard people who are different than us. Our mission should be to learn to identify the similarities between us all so that we can practice empathy with anyone.

Selective empathy is what I experienced with my mother. I had zero emotional intelligence when it came to her. I was just a wild ball of hurt and anger. As is often the case, my anger came from unmet expectations. Many times, we define in advance what role someone is supposed to play in our life, and when they fail to live up to that definition, we judge them and get angry. Empathy helps with this anger because empathy releases us from being reliant on preconceived definitions of a person's role. Instead of defining others' roles in our life based on societal expectations or our personal paradigms, we allow people to simply be themselves. When we stop defining who and what people are supposed to be, we free ourselves from expectations. As expectations disappear, so does judgment.

Empathy ultimately enables forgiveness. I spent years and years disliking my mother until I sat with her for the last two and a half years of her life and watched her die. I was able to see her as Joretta, the human being, someone who had been hurt, someone who had fears, someone who needed love, someone who wanted to feel important and significant. I realized that she was just a person trying to do the best she could. And I could feel her. I felt her sadness. I listened to her, put myself in her position, and understood her world better simply by being in her space and empathizing.

Anytime you find yourself judging someone else, you lack empathy. I don't care what their story is—if they're a murderer, a drug addict, your dad, or the president. If you're judging them and their behavior, then you lack empathy for their journey. You can disagree with their actions and beliefs, but this doesn't mean you should then judge them. We are all more alike than we are different.

Today, I don't harbor any negative feelings toward my mother. I can't even find that old anger. I look at her and think, *Gosh, she was trying the best she could. She had a house full of kids, and she was doing it by herself. She made sure we had great Christmases. She loved making us Easter baskets. She believed in God and introduced others to Christ. She was hardworking, always had two to three jobs. She was independent and feisty and stubborn, and she was such a strong person.* I can have those thoughts now because I choose to look at her through a lens of gratitude and empathy.

EXPANDING EMPATHY

You already know how to be empathetic. At some point in your life, you've felt others' pain and sought to understand their journey. The key to becoming more empathetic is extending your empathy beyond your inner circle of loved ones to everyone in your life and beyond, no matter how different they are or how they might have hurt you in the past. I believe that if success doesn't look like loving the people around you, then you've missed the whole point of life. You can't call yourself a success if you have hate in your heart toward others simply because they're different from you or because they've hurt you.

It's important to find appropriate ways to understand people. One way is to get out of your world and experience other people and things that are different from you. Sometimes people are forced to interact with other cultures and peoples, whether it be at work, in the neighborhood, or at friendly gatherings. However, many people spend their entire lives surrounded by people similar to them. If you're not forced to interact and connect with people different from you, it becomes all the more important for you to go out and make a conscious effort to do so. If you don't, you miss out on the opportunity to better understand other people and their struggles and joys.

You likely know where your empathy gaps are. If there are certain groups you tend to judge or lack empathy for, make an effort to learn more about them. That may just give you the understanding and context necessary to be empathetic.

If you can't interact one-on-one with people from different backgrounds than your own, start by reading a book or watching a movie or documentary that features a different perspective from your status quo paradigm. If you never step outside of your comfort zone and experience things you're not accustomed to, you'll continue operating on your downloaded systems of belief and go into assumption mode.

Other great exercises for expanding empathy are travel and volunteer work. These are great ways to enter spaces outside of your world. I talk about race a lot since it's an issue that affects me and my people personally, but your empathy gap may involve other subgroups—cancer survivors, drug addicts, veterans, illegal immigrants, victims of human trafficking. The possibilities are endless.

Since I resigned from my coaching position, I've had my eyes opened to so many different hurts in the world. I went to a seminar where I listened to stories about human sex trafficking—young girls being kidnapped, forced to consume drugs and alcohol, and sold for sex. I've learned more about how our veterans return home from service and can't mentally conform to civilization. They feel isolated and alone, often turning to drugs and alcohol. After one of my speeches, a young Hispanic man came up to me and told me about how his mom had just been deported three days prior. He was only eighteen, and he now had to figure out a way to support himself and his little brother. Every single person in this world has a story—unseen heartache, hopes and dreams, joys and struggles—but we often are so wrapped up in our own worlds that we don't notice and, even worse, don't care.

Actively seeking to build your empathy for all sorts of different people will build your character and increase your humility. When you work on your empathy, you become more vulnerable, and you widen your perspective of the world. This benefits you as much as it benefits those around you. When you can give your pain perspective and see that you're not alone, it's easier to deal with life when it punches you in the mouth.

TAKE YOUR G AND E VITAMINS

On the most simplistic level, taking daily doses of your G and E vitamins will make you a better, happier person.

Gratitude is how you build your best life from within, by learning to appreciate everything. Being grateful is my happiness formula. Empathy is how you build your best life outside of yourself. It's how you can look at other people nonjudgmentally, without expectations, and learn to accept people as they are.

For me, as a person of faith, I think of gratitude and empathy as our God values. They're all about love—loving other people and loving our lives. When you practice gratitude and empathy daily, you bring love to the table in every circumstance and situation, thus ruling out hate, anger, and negativity.

STATE YOUR CAUSE

To become your best self, you must orient yourself toward growth. You do that by identifying your purpose. We're all here for a reason. Our objective is to find out exactly what that purpose is and then to work toward it every day.

In reality, you will likely have many purposes throughout your life. Some may be defining aspects of your entire life, and others may last only a season. As you change and grow and progress, your purpose will evolve too. For me, I was an athlete one day, then a coach, and now I'm a public speaker and author. I am sure to have many more responsibilities that will force me to adjust my purpose.

Sometimes your purpose might be staring you right in the face, or it might drop into your lap unexpectedly. When I found out my mother was dying, my purpose immediately shifted to being the best daughter I could be. I believe that this was my purpose all along; I was late to embrace it.

Your purpose must be personal to you. Someone else might think my greatest purpose was to be a head basketball coach making $135,000 a year at age thirty-one. But to me, caring for my mother was a greater purpose. I continued coaching, but I made a conscious decision that basketball would not come before my mother—I would not put her on the backburner. Money is nice. Actually, money is great, but money can't buy you a loving relationship with your mother or stop her from dying. Your purpose is what will bring you fulfillment and stretch you into the best version of yourself. Basketball and coaching had helped me grow in many ways, but at this point in my life, my best version of myself had transitioned outside of athletics. My purpose thus had to shift as well. Caring for my mother allowed me to grow and expand in ways that my coaching job could not.

Your purpose must also be something you love or for someone you love. So many people lack an attitude of continual learning not because they are lazy or stupid but because they don't love what they do enough to want to be the best at it.

Adversity can be the thing that leads you to what you

love, because adversity is the birthplace of innovation. Discovery and curiosity are gifts we receive from adversity. The purpose for our life is always greater than the pain of our situation. If your pain is very, very deep, then the purpose of your life is that much greater. Oftentimes your pain and adversity are there to highlight the features that make you special and unique to the world.

PURPOSE IN MY LIFE

As I mentioned previously, I had two saving graces growing up—God and basketball. These were my anchors, keeping me grounded and strong; they were also my sails, lifting me above my circumstances, giving me a reliable sanctuary from the cloud of pain and self-doubt that clung to me in my childhood home.

My mother had her faults, but missing church wasn't one of them. She always made sure we were in church every Sunday and every Wednesday night. I will be eternally grateful for this, because having faith in something greater than myself, faith that God put me on this planet for a reason, for a *purpose*, saved me from drowning in my pain. I first began playing basketball right around the time my mother's husband sexually abused me, and I believe God gave me basketball to save my life, to act as a distraction from the noise.

In February 2009, after my DUI, one of the lowest points of my life, I again latched onto purpose—my goal of being head coach—as a beacon of light in the dark. I had been journaling for a while at that point, because Oprah told me I should, and if Oprah tells me to do something, I'm gonna do it! Three years before my DUI, I had written in my journal that I was ready to become a head coach. Professionally, I was ready to move to that next step, but personally, I wasn't.

Remember what I said in Chapter 3 about "a personal experience of emotional impact" being one of the ways to alter your subconscious? The DUI was one of mine. Immediately, I took responsibility for my behavior and decided that I would be different moving forward. I was determined to maximize my potential as a person and a basketball coach. No longer would I take my gifts for granted. I focused on my purpose. I'd said three years ago that I was ready to be a head coach, and I was finally going to make it happen.

I doubled down on my study of personal development, changed my environment, and got more determined than ever. At the end of that year's basketball season, I began looking for a job as a head coach. I didn't care where I went. I just knew I needed growth, something new. I think we all feel that at various points in our lives. What we're doing isn't working, our behavior isn't sustainable, and it's just a matter of time before life shows us just how much. Our current situation may be dark. A storm may be raging in us or around us. But we *know* that there is something more—something better—waiting for us to come grab it. Oftentimes, it's something that has lived in our heart and mind for years.

At the age of twenty-nine, three months after my DUI arrest, I was offered my first head coaching job at NCAA Division II Tusculum College in Greeneville, Tennessee. I inherited an incredibly talented team that had won championships, and my goal was for us to win a national championship. I spent a wonderful three years there. We won four championships in my three years, and though we didn't get the national championship win I wanted, we got really close.

My DUI forced me to grow and develop on a personal level as well as professionally. My intense focus on my purpose helped me turn my adversity into an advantage. In my case, the old me had to die in order for the new me to be born.

THE PURPOSE OF WORK

We weren't created for work; work was created for us. At various points in history, different individuals didn't like the world as it stood, so they innovated and created.

From Thomas Edison and his light bulb, to Henry Ford and his automobile, to Jeff Bezos and his e-commerce empire—the world is always playing catch-up. When I was growing up, video games "were bad"—"a distraction, a waste of time." Now the video game industry is said to be worth nearly $138 billion. Those kids who were "wasting their time" are making millions of dollars creating video games, improving game technology, selling video games, and even playing video games. They stated their cause and went after it, and the world had to adjust and catch up, creating new jobs and new work. You are not a servant to work. You are the creator of the work.

The world will probably never truly validate what you do. It'll be late to the party—late to understand you. This is why inner work is so important. The outside world won't be able to validate you most of the time, so you must learn to do it for yourself. Tapping into your six higher mental faculties—intuition, will, perception, imagination, reason, and memory—will help you do this. These are the traits that separate us from other animals, and they help us to create and become one with who we really are and who we are intended to be.

When I say "work," I'm not talking about your job or career; I'm talking about something more encompassing. To me, work is obsessive attention toward the most elevated version of yourself that you can imagine. That's what you want to be working toward. Work can be physical. It can be mental. It can be a million different things. Work is any serious, intentional effort toward the truest, greatest version of who you are.

We're told that if we simply work hard, we will find success and be happy. That may have been a reliable formula twenty-five years ago, but I think it's very outdated now. And if you want to talk about hard work, nobody worked harder than slaves. There were probably a lot of scientists, doctors, artists, and entrepreneurs out in those fields and in the masters' homes, but they were not allowed to "state their cause." They were never able to use their adversity to create a new world, to enlarge their thinking of what was possible, and to write their own story.

Success is not a byproduct of working hard. I almost think that the worst thing you can tell somebody is to "just work hard," because that's not enough. You must set goals worthy of your soul.

GOALS WORTHY OF YOUR SOUL

I only want to work hard on things that add value to my various purposes on this planet, because success without fulfillment is failure.

Fulfillment comes from pursuing your dreams. Most

people don't pursue their dreams, for a variety of reasons. Sometimes, instead of looking inward to find our dreams, we look to the outside world. We pursue goals based on what will get us the most applause or make us "successful" by society's standards.

Sometimes other people's dreams for us are imposed onto us. You and I both know people who receive a lot of familial pressure to go to college, join the military, join the family business, attend law school, become doctors, or conform to whatever image their family has of them. They may want to become something else, but their family's expectations are so ingrained that they follow the expected path. As a result, they end up unfulfilled and unhappy. That's not success to me, because they're not doing what they've been put here to do. They're living someone else's dream and story.

Pursuing a goal that is worthy of your soul will energize you. It will give you the strength and will to keep going in the midst of setbacks and challenges. If you're doing something that moves you and totally excites you from the inside out, then your dream is aligned with whom you were created to be. The goals that move you from the inside-out allow you to persist. I can demonstrate incredible persistence in the life I want to live, but if you wanted me to be an accountant, I would quit very quickly.

We all have different skills, and we're all unique. There's

never going to be another *you*, and there's never going to be another *me*. We're all put here for a reason. I'm an extrovert for a reason. I'm good at one skill and not another one for a reason.

We all have different strengths because the universe has a goal and a dream for us. Oprah talks about how your job is to lean into the dream the universe has for you. To discover this dream, listen to your intuition. Your intuition—your gut feeling—is the universe's prayer to you. The closer you can align with the universe's dream for you, the brighter you'll shine.

WHAT'S MORE IMPORTANT THAN HARD WORK

I don't want to diminish the value of hard work. You *do* need to work hard. The greatest book ever written says, "Faith without works is dead" (James 2:26 KJV). However, it is not the only indicator of success and is not even the most important one. There are three things more important than your work ethic: finding what you're good at, utilizing your vision and imagination, and attacking fear.

FIND WHAT YOU'RE GOOD AT

First, find the things you're good at, and go all in on them. This is one of the places where you should go deep instead of wide and shallow. Tyler Perry said on *Oprah's Master*

Class, "Find the one thing you do well and master it. It will afford you the opportunity to do all of the other things."

That idea resonated with me when I heard it, because it's exactly what I did. I started as a player and worked to master that. Then, because of my mastery as a player, I was able to become a coach. Then I worked to be the best coach I could be. Now, I've taken my mastery as a coach and funneled it into public speaking and personal development, where just like when I was a coach, I communicate, inspire, and help people enlarge their vision of what's possible. The fundamental skills have remained the same; I've simply pivoted to a new medium. When you achieve mastery in one thing, doors will open for you to use your talents and skills to do other things. Your eyes will open to more opportunities to use your gifts.

Sometimes it takes time to discover what you're good at. Ask yourself, "What moves me from the inside out?" I could work twenty straight hours on basketball. As a coach, I could stay in that environment and not see the time at all. Monday would turn into Friday before I even realized it. When you're operating within your gifts, time is invisible. It's not hard work; it's *heart* work, and that's the best place to live.

Once you find what you're good at, work to make that

thing the primary focus of your time and energy. Some-times that means temporarily doing something you're not good at in order to get closer to the thing you *are* good at. As long as you're consistently moving toward your unique talents and gifts, you're on the right track.

VISION AND IMAGINATION

You must have a North Star. You need something you really want to go after, an image of yourself being, doing, and having the life you desire—something you can hold in your heart and mind. When you pursue a cause like that, you are aligned in body, mind, and spirit.

Imagination is a great gift. It allows us to envision the future and see things before they happen. Imagination is how we turn our ideas into reality. We imagine something, and then with our intentional action we bring it into being. Our imagination *creates* the future. And the best part? Our imagination is limitless. How big can you dream? How clear can you make those details in your head?

The more detailed and extensive your vision, the more likely it is to come true. Meditation, visualization, and vision boards, as described in Chapter 3, can be useful strategies in pursuing your cause. When you cut an image out and put it on your vision board or document your vision in some way, that idea of who you want to be becomes frozen in time. It becomes a permanent fixture, unaffected by the ticking of the clock, always there for you to refer back to it.

ATTACK FEAR

I don't think we talk about fear enough. Fear can paralyze us, preventing us from ever trying. We stop evolving and surrender to the way things are: the security of a check every two weeks, the boyfriend who has always been there, the town where we've always lived.

I don't care if you're Oprah Winfrey, Michael Jordan, or Adell Harris. It doesn't matter who you are or what role you play in this world—you will be afraid when you go into an unfamiliar space. But truly successful people, people who get results, go anyway. Anyone who desires greatness and growth will come to the crossroads of failure a lot. In the face of fear, you must continue forward.

You must come up with your own definition of fear. For me, fear means "Go! You're right where you need to be, doing the thing that's going to move you closer to your vision." Quick, decisive action is vitally important. Don't sit on your decisions. Successful people, particularly people who reach the level of mastery in their fields, do not take all day to make a decision. They have the ability to evaluate a situation and quickly take action. The sooner you make a decision, the sooner you get results. Decide and go!

Forest Whitaker said on *Inside the Actors Studio*, "Fear pushes me hardcore. It drives me. As opposed to looking at fire as something that burns, I see it as the light that guides me to a higher level."

In a similar vein, I believe that fear is a bridge from where you are to where you want to go. The bridge might feel like a tightrope at times and you might feel like you're going to die, but it's necessary to traverse it to reach your goals. This is one of the reasons you must have a cause worthy of your soul. The thing at the other end of the bridge must be worth it to make you cross through the fear. Your cause must be greater than your fear. For instance, it's usually easier for me to go all in on something, even if I'm afraid, when I know it will improve the lives of others.

Another empowering definition of fear is that if you're not afraid, then you shouldn't be doing it. If something doesn't make you uncomfortable, it means you've already done it before or you already know you can do it. The goal is to reach and do things that you don't know you can do. Fear is the beacon that guides you to the things that will challenge you and change your life.

We all have ambitions, but most people stay where they

are, in their limited lives, because they don't believe their abilities will match their ambitions. But how can you possibly know if you never test your limits?

Fear is normal. Your natural instinct is to protect yourself from the disappointment and pain of failure, but you have to stretch the runway of what's possible. Fear is one of the greatest obstacles you will face, and if you can attack it, you can create a new way of life and become the best, most elevated version of yourself.

OBSTACLES

Four primary obstacles will keep you from orienting toward growth and pursuing your cause: fear of failure, fear of change, feeling of isolation, and lack of confidence.

FEAR OF FAILURE

Fear of failure largely stems from our concern about what others think. You can't be afraid to fail in front of other people. On *Inside the Actors Studio*, Mark Wahlberg talked about his life growing up in Boston and how he initially hid his acting aspirations. Being an actor was less admirable than being a tough guy, and he knew the guys in the neighborhood would laugh at him. Eventually, though, he got to a point where he asked himself, "Why do I care what these guys think of me?"

There will always be people who criticize you. People criticized me as a basketball player. They criticized me as a coach. They criticize me now for quitting my job and taking the next step in my journey. They criticize me for opening up about my childhood. "What the hell are you doing? Why would you share those things about your mom's personal life? Why would you leave college athletics? How are you gonna make a living talking to people?" they ask.

Those people don't matter. Public opinion is overrated, and self-confidence is uncommon. Don't accept the world's view of failure; create your own philosophy. If you fail, that failure is yours; it's not anyone else's. No one else gets permission to count your losses or wins. You're the only person qualified to decide what failure means for you. All failure means for me is that one thing I tried didn't work. There's always another step, a new approach, I can take.

It's okay to fail. The more you try, the more you'll fail, because you're testing new things. Each failure is an experience that helps you map your next steps. Failure is not an indicator that you should quit; it's simply an indicator that it's time to change your approach or be patient.

FEAR OF CHANGE

As I've already mentioned, change is scary. But loyalty to

your old paradigms, your old way of thinking, and your old environment is limiting.

There's going to be change. If you've decided to rewrite your story, you've already signed up for that. You've decided that the current status quo isn't good enough.

Even though change is scary, deep down, you *want* change to happen. Focus on what you want and why you want it. Your why will keep you excited about achieving your goal.

FEELING ISOLATED

As you grow into a new version of yourself and pursue new goals, other people may not understand. You might feel that you're letting other people down.

We all want to be liked and accepted by others, but your journey of growth may push you into a different place in your life. As you leave old paradigms behind, you may also have to break away from those around you who are still living from those paradigms.

This can feel isolating but remember: this journey is about you. You can't live your life based on the opinions of others.

Also, even though you may feel alone, you're not. Many

other people have gone through the exact same feeling. Seek out models to remind yourself that others have experienced the same feeling of isolation and worked through it.

Then, as you grow, you will naturally expand your network, finding new people who are "goal getters," eliminating the feeling of isolation. You will attract the right people that align with your new vibration.

LACK OF CONFIDENCE

You won't get anything done without confidence and a strong belief in yourself. I encourage you to dream big—shockingly big. Your dreams should be so outrageous that they sound ridiculous to anyone else but you. Then you must believe that you can accomplish those dreams. One of my favorite sayings is "Believing is seeing." When you believe something will happen, you will see it happen. If you don't believe you can achieve something, then of course you won't achieve it.

Confidence goes hand in hand with the law of attraction, which states that you will attract whatever you focus your energy on. Some people interpret the law of attraction to mean that if you want something bad enough, you'll get it. The law of attraction is about more than just wanting something, though. It's about wanting something and *intentionally affirming that you have it, in advance of its physical manifestation.* It's about focusing all of your thoughts and energy on your desired outcome.

When you have confidence and faith in your abilities and truly believe you can accomplish your desired goal, you begin to vibrate at the frequency of that goal. When you are connected to your goal in this way, you unlock a well of energy that will empower you to take the actions needed to achieve the goal. This is how you will "attract" your desired outcome.

If you lack confidence, it's like trying to play basketball with one hand tied behind your back: you're going to be at a severe disadvantage. A lack of confidence is all about perception, though. By rewriting your story, you can work to grow into a more confident individual.

OVERCOMING THE OBSTACLES: BE COURAGEOUS!

These four obstacles—fear of failure, fear of change, feeling of isolation, and lack of confidence—won't disappear on their own. But instead of looking at them as things holding you back, look at them as indicators of opportunity—chances for growth.

Courage is what counteracts fear, so to face and push through these obstacles, you will be required to act courageously. It takes courage both to begin and to sustain the journey. Every time you face a setback or fall back into old patterns, you will need to draw on your courage once more.

Anything that requires you to step outside of your old belief system and habits will require bravery, but many of us struggle to be brave. We think, *I'm not a courageous person, so how am I supposed to do this? Where do I find my courage?*

This is part of your story you have to rewrite. We are all courageous. It is in our spiritual DNA. Sometimes we just don't access our courage until we're given no other option. Don't wait for life to force you to be courageous. Draw on the strength you've shown against past adversity and *choose* to be courageous.

THE POINT OF STATING YOUR CAUSE

When we die, our gravestone is engraved with our birth date, a dash, and our death date. Your cause is that dash in the middle. Linda Ellis's book *Live Your Dash* communicates this message beautifully. Your cause is what you choose to do with your life.

Explicitly stating your cause makes it more real. I try to state my cause—what I'm here to do and how I'm going to do it—at least five times a day. Every time I say it, it becomes even more a part of who I am, and I align myself with the vibration of the cause, which will help me stay on track to becoming who the universe wants me to be.

Stating your cause gives you the energy to keep pushing forward. When you look at people who have gone through adversity after adversity, you may wonder how they keep getting up. It's because of their cause. They have something greater than their pain, something more important than any setback, something aligned with what the universe dreamed for them. That cause gives them the energy to keep going.

For your cause to be strong enough to overcome all your obstacles, you must offer your gifts and talents to something greater than yourself. That's the overall objective: to add value to the world. Maybe that means contributing to a relationship, a team, your workplace, or your community.

Our gifts and talents were designed for something greater than ourselves, but it's up to us to figure out what that greater purpose is. For Martin Luther King, it was to lead the civil rights movement. For Steve Jobs, it was innovating and creating new products. Look at your models and study the ripple effect of value that they've added to the world. What do you want to leave behind? It's okay if you don't know yet, but you should be actively searching for your purpose, because you don't have forever to figure it out.

Stating your cause will attract the right people and opportunities. That's the law of attraction. You get a clear idea of what you want, who you want to become, and how you're going to do it. You journal, master your language daily, visualize using your vision board, meditate, and model the people you admire. You state your cause aloud and consistently direct your thoughts in that direction.

Perhaps you want to be a doctor or a great mother or a singer. Whatever it is, when you focus all your attention on that thing, you begin operating on a new level. You increase your energy and tune into the right frequency. You put positive vibrations out into the world, and you attract positive things back. You will meet people who add value to your journey, and doors will open up for you that maybe wouldn't have opened up before. You're no longer working independently; you are co-creating with the universe.

Your cause is the key to ensuring your mind, body, and spirit are in alignment with the universe. Once you state your cause, let it guide your decisions. Let your dream run the show. In November 2011, I decided that my cause was to be the best daughter I could be. Because I had already stated my cause and established who I was going to be, I didn't need to make any more decisions; I let my cause guide me and make my decisions for me until the end of my mother's life.

Stating your cause brings balance to your life, because your cause is your foundation—the driving force of your life.

HOW TO FIND AND STATE YOUR CAUSE

To find your cause, take inventory regularly. We are constantly evolving, and our cause can change too. Anytime you feel you are in a new season of your life, perform a self-audit.

Ask yourself these questions:

- What do I want from life? Am I getting it? If not, why not?
- What do I do well? What do I do better than most with less effort? What would I do for free?
- How can I best serve others? How can I use my talents to do that?
- What are my challenges here to teach me?
- Are my thoughts and actions aligned with my cause(s)/ goal(s)? Do my goals and dreams make my decisions for me?

I recommend writing down your answers to these questions. Anytime you feel yourself losing sight of your cause, read through your responses.

I also recommend regularly revisiting these questions as your life changes. New challenges will arise, and the people around you will have different needs. Maybe your significant other gets fired. Perhaps your best friend's mother dies, or someone you love gets sick. How can you best serve these people in these new situations?

In addition to regularly revisiting these core questions, I recommend asking yourself every single day, "What action can I take right now that can get me closer to my cause? What can I do today, in this moment?" This will ensure that you are taking concrete steps toward your cause.

STATING YOUR CAUSE IN THE DIFFERENT ROLES OF YOUR LIFE

Stating your cause is closely linked to being clear on who you are in all spheres of your life. You will have a cause as an individual, as a member of your family, as a professional, and as a member of your community.

Your cause as an individual is about who you want to be, as a man or woman. How do you want to behave? What kind of attitude do you want to have?

For your cause as a member of your family, what kind of a parent/child/sibling do you want to be? What do you want your familial relationships to look like? (Note that "family" is whatever you want to define it as here. If you don't have close relationships with your biological family, you can still have close friends or mentors who are like family to you.)

Your cause as a professional is your cause as it relates to your job or career. This is where you begin to move outside of your home life and focus on your contribution to others. What kind of student do you want to be? What kind of contribution are you going to make at your workplace? What role are you going to play on your team?

Finally, your cause within your community is how you give back to the world. Do you want to volunteer? Do you want to share your story to help others feel less alone? Do you want to provide some service to the community?

THE IMPORTANCE OF BALANCE

Naturally, there will be a lot of overlap between the different spheres because you will be utilizing the same gifts and talents in each. However, by explicitly stating your cause in each area of your life, you can ensure balance and prevent one aspect of your life from taking over. True happiness and fulfillment comes from balance across the spheres.

Back in my twenties, I was thriving in my career and community spheres. I was experiencing great success as a coach and was helping support my players as young women, but I was struggling in my individual and family spheres. I was self-medicating with alcohol and food, I was twenty pounds overweight, and I wasn't happy with my relationship with my mother. Finding success in two out of four spheres may seem pretty good, but it led me to a DUI and a dark spiral of sadness and anger.

You must state your cause in each sphere so that you can ensure that area of your life will get the attention it needs. By explicitly stating your goals in each sphere, you become clear on what values you have to adopt in order to support your vision—you can begin to make a plan of action.

For example, maybe you want to build the biggest company in downtown New York, but you also want to be an excellent father. Once you state you want to be an excellent father, you know that one of your values must be spending time with your children and building the biggest company must happen in conjunction with time with your kids. Create a workable plan that matches your goal—it's really that simple. Your plan doesn't need to be incredibly detailed. In this context, "plan" simply means increased awareness. Your plan is basically figuring out the destination and then slowly filling in the holes with information.

Then, when you face challenges, like whether to go to your daughter's softball game or stay late at the office, you already have the values and plan in place to help you make your decision.

The ultimate goal is to gain clarity on a single, all-encompassing self-image that extends into each category. There's no separation between me the person, me the sister, me the CEO and entrepreneur, and me the public speaker motivating my community. All those roles are connected to my self-image as a servant leader. It doesn't matter if I'm with family, in a workspace, or in my community, I strive to be someone who adds positive value to everyone I meet.

REPETITION

Who you want to become is a lifelong journey. It never ends. You're going to want to become something, and then you'll reach that level and realize that you can grow and achieve even more. As my business mentor says, "Finished never is."

You're going to want a job badly, and then you're going to get that job, and you'll think, *Okay, I'm here. Now I want a raise.* Or, *Now I want a promotion.* Or, *Now I want another job.* You gain more experience, knowledge, and awareness, and thus become more qualified and more confident.

Once the mind experiences something, it can't go back to its original form. You can't become a millionaire and then act like you don't know what it's like to be a millionaire. The world's different from that point on. Your opportunities, goals, and beliefs are different.

That's why you should continue to take inventory and evaluate your cause in all the various spheres of your life. Do it weekly, monthly, or annually—however often you need to stay focused on where you want to go.

Remember to give yourself permission to change your mind. There is no reason to be loyal to your old paradigms. If you're still making the same decisions you did ten years ago, that shows a lack of growth, not loyalty. When it's time to evolve—time to do something else—listen to your intuition and be ready to take the needed calculated risks.

STATE YOUR CAUSE

Your purpose is how you use your gifts to contribute to something greater than yourself. Sometimes your purpose might be an ambitious, lifelong pursuit to enact great change in the world, and sometimes your purpose might be commitment to improve a single person's life in a finite way. All causes, no matter how big or small they seem, are consequential and meaningful. Any effort you expend to improve the world is effort well spent.

Though your specific purpose may change throughout your life, the benefits of stating your cause remain the same. Finding your purpose provides direction, keeps you motivated, teaches you perspective, and gives you the feeling that all your work is worth it.

SHARE YOUR STORY

Sharing allows us to express our feelings and experiences, and sharing connects us with others. As human beings, we are desperately looking for ways to express who we are. I believe we find our unique talents and gifts in these moments of discovery. Everything we do is an attempt to express who we are or what's happening within us—the clothes we wear, the car we drive, the house we live in, the music we listen to, the books we read, the God we worship, the people we associate with, and the list goes on and on. Remember, the body is an instrument of the mind, and we cannot truly make adversity our advantage until we embrace all that we are and find healthy ways to express ourselves.

Music reminds me that honest, vulnerable, and authentic storytelling is at the heart of all human connection. In the movie *8 Mile*, Eminem's character B-Rabbit raps, "I am white, I am a fucking bum / I do live in a trailer with my mum." If you've seen the movie, you know that it took some time for B-Rabbit to arrive at this place of full disclosure. Choosing to embrace who he was empowered him and also made him relatable to the masses. Using hip-hop music as his vehicle, Eminem made his way out of that double-wide trailer, becoming one of the world's most celebrated artists. I'm not saying that you will become the next Eminem, but I am saying that people identify with the truth.

When you share your story with the world, you're free like B-Rabbit in *8 Mile*. Free from embarrassment, shame, and guilt about who you truly are. Free to become all that you were destined to be. We hide because we fear we won't be accepted and loved for who we truly are. This fear limits us and forces us into unhealthy forms of self-expression—alcoholism, drug use, obsession with status or wealth and material possessions, sexual abuse, domestic violence, murder, racism, sexism, overeating, or just being a bad human being. You can embrace and express your truth, and become unapologetically yourself, which empowers you and allows others to see themselves in your truth.

Sharing your story requires vulnerability. There are few things I respect more than people who show vulnerability, as vulnerability requires you to demonstrate boldness despite the fear of not being accepted. Such authentic, courageous vulnerability is, in fact, a strength, and it is where your magic lies. Showing vulnerability empowers others, whether you are Martin Luther King Jr. saying "I am a black man, I deserve to be treated equally, and I refuse to back down or go away" or you are Oprah Winfrey saying "I am a woman doing the same job as a man, and I deserve to be compensated accordingly" or you are Adell Harris saying "I have been rejected, abused, and abandoned. I have drunk myself to sleep more nights than I care to admit. I've been depressed and suicidal. I've felt unworthy of love and alone, but, just like you, my purpose is greater than my pain. I will never surrender to the circumstances of my past; I will gladly embrace every step of my journey and encourage others to do the same."

In expressing yourself, you can be a light that illuminates the world. You show people that they are not alone and that they too can make adversity their advantage.

The ongoing process of making adversity your advantage isn't complete without expressing yourself. All the steps of the process have a purpose, and this final step is very important. If you skip this last step, you'll miss the part where you find joy in your journey.

Full expression of yourself is liberating and empowering. By releasing all that you've kept locked inside, you will find peace in your new story—the story where you're the hero and no longer the victim or villain. There's power in your story, and it is only through rewriting and sharing with others that you can unleash its full power.

HOW I'VE SHARED MY STORY

Sharing your story is a process of self-discovery. It takes time. Your life has chapters, and each chapter will have its share of adversity. Some chapters are more intense than others, but in every chapter, you must transition past the physical moment in order to evaluate that chapter's spiritual and intellectual effects on who you are. It took me going through a full cycle of personal and professional adversity, evaluation, and growth to understand myself better. I call these cycles growth spurts, and as long as I live, I'll have them, because "finished never is." In each phase of my life, I've found the courage to learn and embrace more of myself, hence allowing me to share more of myself. In my most recent growth spurt, I found the courage to write this book, sharing my full story. Before that, I had only shared parts of my story with my friends, my associates, and the young women I coached.

Now I've shared my story with ten times the number of people I'd shared it with prior to my last growth spurt. I stand up in front of large groups of people, and I tell them that at the age of eight I was sexually abused by my mom's second husband. I tell them that I blamed my mother for my pain and spent a decade hating her. I tell them that I resorted to alcohol when my grandmother died of lung cancer and that I was depressed and that there were times I didn't think my life was worth living. When I share my truth, I empower myself. The people, circumstances, and events I've endured might be ugly and dark, but I don't have to be ugly and dark.

Every time I get up and speak my truth, my hope is that someone will find a parallel in something I say. It might be that we're both women or that we're both black or that we were both sexually abused. Perhaps someone in the audience was adopted like me or gay like me. Maybe someone else also had a friend that committed suicide or had a father that didn't want a relationship with him or her. There are so many layers in my story that might help someone.

By choosing to be vulnerable, I empower the people who are listening, just like Oprah did for me. As a young adult, I was looking for representation and inclusion. I never knew that there were other people that had experienced what I had. I thought I was alone, but then other people's courage to be vulnerable proved me wrong. Vulnerability shows us that we are all sharing the same human experience.

SHARING KILLS SHAME

Shame and guilt imprison and suffocate us. A lack of self-acceptance and feelings of embarrassment lead to an internal battle that manifests outwardly in the form of depression, addiction, suicide, and other self-destructive behavior. Shame subconsciously seeks consequence. When we feel like we've done something wrong, our paradigm/belief system takes over and tells us that there must be a consequence. As long as we feel shame and guilt, we often will punish ourselves without even realizing we're doing it. This is why some people who experienced sexual abuse will overeat to obesity or why someone who's suffered the public embarrassment of falling from a high-profile job or financial status will go into a deep depression and might even become suicidal. Shame and guilt are lonely, hopeless places to be.

I've experienced a lot of guilt and shame in my life. As a young girl, I was ashamed of my body; I matured faster than my peers and, as a result, received unwanted attention from older guys. I was ashamed of what my mother's husband did to me. I was ashamed of the dysfunction taking place in my home. I've felt both shame and guilt that my father didn't want a relationship with me. For most of my life, I was ashamed of my sexuality. Being raised in the South and in the black church, I was taught that being gay would have me burning in the flames of hell for eternity. If that doesn't make you feel guilty, I'm not sure what would. But more than guilt tactics and judgment from the church, my fear of being abandoned, rejected, and unloved was suffocating. I'm also ashamed of how I treated my mother in my twenties. She deserved better from me.

Self-acceptance should be taught in every home and school. Embracing your truth, despite how ugly it is or how other people may view you, is a mandatory step to making adversity your advantage. The more you communicate who you are, the more self-acceptance you'll develop, and self-acceptance kills shame and guilt. This is why sharing is a key aspect of rehabilitation therapy. Although I haven't personally participated in such meetings, I know that a key part of closed Alcoholics Anonymous meetings is stating aloud that you are an alcoholic: "Hi, my name is _____, and I'm an alcoholic." The meeting creates a safe, judgment-free zone for alcoholics to embrace who they are, leading to personal empowerment. By communicating who you are aloud, scars and all, you accept the whole of your being and thus shed your shame and guilt. When you share your story, you can judge the events of your story, but you don't judge yourself.

Expressing who you are authentically is empowering. I grow a little taller every time I speak or share my story. My shoulders go back, and I stand up straighter. Whether you're expressing your story to one person or to one mil-

lion people, it's empowering because it gets you closer
to understanding, accepting, and loving yourself. This
continual journey of learning to love yourself more opens
you to loving others more fully, as it is only when you love
yourself that you can love others.

SHARING DRIVES GROWTH

Sharing your story opens your eyes to the courage and
strength you've shown. How strong are you? As strong as
you've had to be. Sharing your story forces you to reflect
on who you are and how far you've come. You'll be sur-
prised how liberating this will be for your spirit.

Sharing your story also leads to further reflection and
increased awareness. When you speak your story aloud or
communicate it to someone else, something may jump out
at you that you didn't consider previously. Because we are
constantly evolving, it's common for us to know something
from one point of view and see it completely differently
later in life. Who we are isn't who we'll always be. The
understanding that I am constantly growing and evolving
has oftentimes been exactly what I needed to keep going.

Jay-Z—the greatest hip-hop artist ever, in my opinion—
said, "You can't heal what you never reveal."

We all have a natural ability to heal, physically as well

as emotionally. However, the intensity of the hurt dictates the extent to which your body or mind can heal itself on its own. If you get a minor scrape, for example, the wound will heal quickly and easily, no doctor's visit needed. If you break your arm, though, and you don't go to the doctor to have it set, the arm could heal improperly, leaving you with other issues. And if you receive a cancer diagnosis, you will have to return to the doctor regularly to receive treatment.

Sharing your story is to emotional healing what going to the doctor is to physical healing. Some emotional hurts heal on their own, but others require you to share your story. Remember that adversity, just like cancer, kills if left unattended. As Jay-Z said, in order to heal, the hurt must be revealed. You do that by sharing your true story.

It's incredibly powerful to know and embrace exactly who you are. Forward movement comes from accepting who you are *today*, starting from where you are, and moving forward. By sharing your story and accepting all of yourself, you prime yourself for further growth. All your hopes, dreams, desires, and wishes require growth to happen. If you always do what you've always done, you'll always get what you've always got. Growth is the key ingredient that will break this cycle and allow you to get more out of life.

The overall growth you experience from sharing will also

open up new opportunities. A world opens to you that never existed before. By sharing your story, you become clear about who you are and what you want. You release the baggage and clear the fog of everything that's in the way and stopping you from forward movement. You will then attract the right people and the right opportunities into your life, because opportunities only present themselves when you become the person ready to receive them. These opportunities might be career-based, relationship-based, or family-based.

As Jim Rohn said, "We don't get what we want, we get what we are. To earn more, we must become more."

SHARING SERVES THE WORLD

Serving the world is our duty. We all should use our talents, gifts, experiences, and knowledge to help others. If you've accomplished anything, I believe that it is your responsibility to share how you did it.

It's my personal mission to impact the life of everybody I come into contact with in a positive way. I had several early influences that emphasized giving and sharing. My first coach, Dana Conte, did much more than he was required or expected to do. He shared his time and his knowledge with me, and that served in a meaningful way in my life. He was a huge influence and left a lasting impact on me. My personal philosophy on service originated from my unique upbringing.

My mother also showed me the importance of helping others. Because of her incredible example, the only environment I ever knew growing up was that you were supposed to help people. She dedicated much of her life to raising children who weren't hers. Some of these kids later expressed to me how this gesture had changed their lives. She shared her faith and her home with kids who had no one, and in doing so, she gave back to the world.

If you've suffered layers of adversity or trauma, sharing your story can improve the lives of others who may be going through similar issues. The way you share your story is up to you. Sometimes you may explicitly share the adversities you've experienced, and other times, you may simply share your space and your life with others, as Dana and my mother did.

I coached fourteen years, and every single year, at least one player shared with me that she'd been sexually abused, leading to other issues with self-acceptance and self-worth. Some suffered body image issues leading to eating disorders like anorexia and bulimia. Others struggled with cutting, alcoholism, sexually promiscuity, or anger management issues. These girls were young people just like me that were hurting, with their unattended wounds manifesting into toxic behaviors.

For many of these girls, I was the first person in their lives in a position of leadership who told them, "I was sexually abused, too." While I couldn't heal their wounds for them, I was able to show them that they weren't alone in their experiences. I was able to show them that others had faced the same struggles and succeeded in making adversity their advantage. I was also able to offer them tools and strategies for whenever they were ready to address their pain.

We are so much more connected than we realize. One of my favorite passages from President Barack Obama's book *The Audacity of Hope* says, "We have a stake in one another, and that which binds us together is greater than what drives us apart, and if enough people believe in the truth of that proposition and act on it, then we might not solve every problem, but we can get something meaningful done for the people with whom we share this Earth." In order for us to find those binding connections, we must be willing to share our truth and embrace other people's differences. So, don't underestimate what sharing your story could do for someone else.

HOW TO SHARE

Obviously, I'm sharing my story in this book, but you don't have to write a book to share your story. (I do believe, though, that everyone should write a book, even if it's just for their kids, grandkids, and great-grandkids.) Your life matters and can be a model for others that you might never meet. You don't need a public platform to share your story. The greatest platform can be a one-on-one conversation with someone you love.

You don't need to stand up in front of dozens of people and share your story; you just need to express yourself in a way that is truthful, authentic, and empowering. And if you want to share your story with a larger audience, we all have access to the internet. You can start your own YouTube channel, write a blog, or even post to social media to share your message.

I advise that you be intentional about how you express yourself, because you should share your story in a way that isn't toxic or negative to others. If you're haphazard in your communication, you may say something that is hurtful, or you may express yourself in a way that's not empowering for you or anyone else.

The idea of sharing your story may seem scary and daunting, but we naturally want to express ourselves. Ever had that "I feel like I'm going to explode" feeling? Or what about feeling like you need to have a good cry? Or are you "tough," never giving yourself permission to cry? This used to be me. If never crying were normal, we wouldn't feel the need to proclaim our victory over it. We want to be understood.

On the finale of *The Oprah Winfrey Show*, Oprah said, "I've talked to nearly 30,000 people on this show, and all 30,000 had one thing in common: They all wanted validation. If I could reach through this television and sit on your sofa or sit on a stool in your kitchen right now, I would tell you that every single person you will ever meet shares that common desire. They want to know: 'Do you see me? Do you hear me? Does what I say mean anything to you?'"

We want to share who we are. We want people to listen, and we want to know that what we're saying matters. We simply need to find the avenues to share.

PERSONAL RELATIONSHIPS

Communication is absolutely critical in personal relationships. Seek to share your story with family members, friends, and mentees.

I hope things will be different for future generations, but I was raised in an environment where we didn't have conversations about pain and adversity. We really didn't have conversations at all, but that's another book. All the traumas I experienced up until my early twenties, when my grandmother passed away, were never discussed. I desperately needed someone to talk to about my dysfunctional home and about my best friend committing suicide, but those simply weren't things people talked about, not in the home, at church, or at school.

Fake perfection has hurt us as a society. Too often stigmas are attached to certain topics, and we brush things under the rug for the sake of a perfect image. Fortunately, we as individuals can drive positive change in this regard, starting with our personal relationships and our truth.

For most kids, parents are their first role models. That's why it's so important that parents sit down with their kids and truthfully discuss the mistakes they've made and their history with fear, shame, and embarrassment. The best thing a mom or dad can say is, "You know what? I screwed up in school, too. There was a time I was hanging around the wrong crowd, and I made some decisions that produced severe consequences." Sharing that information requires vulnerability, but being vulnerable doesn't make you less of a parent; it makes you a better parent and a normal human being. It helps your kids understand you better, and it builds trust and strengthens the lines of communication. When your kids go through something, they'll know they have an outlet, someone that won't judge them for making mistakes. If it's not you, it'll be someone else.

When you learn to make adversity your advantage, you become an incredible resource for your friends. Friends frequently share information with each other, but it often becomes a complaining fest. Many people, especially when they're young, don't have the self-awareness or tools to pull themselves out of the victim mentality. Once you begin to master the refuse-to-lose process, you are uniquely qualified to help your friends in ways that most people can't. Perhaps you have a friend who's had a miscarriage or who is going through a divorce or who has lost a job. You can sit down with that friend and share how your own adversities negatively impacted your thoughts and behaviors and explain what you did to move past your old paradigms and rewrite your story. Remember, though, that you can only help people who want to help themselves.

You are also uniquely positioned to become a mentor. If you've experienced success and you don't share it, you're doing the world a disservice. When you make it to the top floor, you need to send the elevator back down. Sometimes, when we go through difficult, painful things, we minimize the experience once we pass through it and no longer want to talk about it. But if you've learned how to make your adversity your advantage, that is a type of success that *must* be shared. Send the elevator back down and help transform another person's life.

PROFESSIONAL RESOURCES

When you need to talk with someone and don't have friends or family who are qualified to help, many traditional professional resources are available to you. Part of owning your outcome is recognizing when you need help and then seeking that help out, be it in the form of a psychologist, therapist, counselor, personal development coach, or spiritual advisor.

Your health insurance may cover such therapy, or if you're a student, your school should provide some form of mental health service. There are also nonprofits that provide this help for free or at a low cost.

The best thing about sharing your story with a professional is that he or she will be completely unbiased and won't judge you. The primary thing stopping us from sharing who we are is usually fear of judgment. We crave acceptance. Professional therapy provides a safe environment to share your story.

It can still take courage to go to therapy, though, especially depending on your community and your programmed beliefs. In the black community, for example, we tend to not talk about anything because historically we *couldn't* talk about our deep pains. We never had a platform, and it was almost never to our advantage to communicate how much pain we were going through. In many cases, voicing our hurts resulted in direct negative consequences. So we just prayed about everything instead, or we expressed ourselves in what we now call "black culture." We prayed about slavery, and we prayed about civil rights. Still today many black people don't go to therapy because this survival tactic of silence has persisted through the generations.

Though many people, black people especially, have been conditioned to a paradigm that looks down on therapy, that paradigm is changing. It is becoming more acceptable for all of us to seek help. Mental health is now recognized as an important aspect of health that needs to be addressed. For example, in Jay-Z's last album 4:44 he talks about the benefits of going to therapy. He grew up in Brooklyn, New York, in the Marcy Projects, at the height of the crack epidemic. Images were painted on the walls of his mind, and old beliefs were deep in his subconscious mind, making growth impossible. Jay-Z, the husband and father, needed to heal, but his past was in the way. As a black man, his open discussion of going to therapy has helped to normalize the idea of therapy in the black community.

Therapy can offer you clarity on who you are, what's happening in your world, and how to become the best version of yourself, especially if you find a good therapist. So go!

OUTSIDE WORLD

The internet has given us an incredible opportunity to communicate with the outside world. I have a strong internet presence. I have a website, make YouTube videos, write a blog, and post on social media for my company, Refuse to Lose. Whenever I click "Submit" or "Post," the content is sent out into the world, and I can't take it back. It's out of my hands, and so it feels like a burden is lifted from my shoulders.

The great thing about sharing your story online—through social media, a blog, YouTube, whatever—is that many of the people who will read or listen to your story will be people who don't know you. Since you don't know them, it doesn't matter what they think, and so you don't have to worry about judgment.

And when you share online with people who do know you, the communication isn't face-to-face. Sharing your story face-to-face with someone can be intimidating and scary, especially if you grew up in an environment like mine, where you never had those kinds of conversations. The distance that the online medium provides can be very welcome. It gives you the space to compose your thoughts and really think about what you want to say, and it allows you to be more in control of the conversation.

Sometimes people will respond negatively, with judgment or rejection. They may not approve of you communicating your truth openly or being who you are. This is one of the times where you must select who you do and do not spend time on. When someone doesn't want you to share your truth, make use of the "Block," "Unfriend," and "Unfollow" buttons. If you receive negative comments from strangers, you need to delete those comments and people from all of your social media platforms. Remember: you don't know those people, and their opinions don't matter.

In my experience, though, most people *will* champion you and support you. Most people have a desire to express some truth of their own, so when they see someone with the courage to be vulnerable, they respect it. Just one person telling you, "Thanks for sharing—I think this can really help a lot of people!" is enough to liberate you and assure you that your story matters.

TIPS FOR SHARING

The most important thing to remember when sharing your story is that you should only go as far as you want to go. Whatever you're sharing should feel good to you. Share as little or as much of your story as you want. You can tell one person or a thousand. Even if you only share a portion of your story with one person, that can be enough to transform that person's life. If you change just one person's life for the better in your lifetime, you have lived a good and meaningful life.

Sharing and communicating are definitely worth it. It's therapeutic to communicate who you are. It's therapeutic to share your dreams and fears out loud. If you are sharing for personal healing, it's worth the risk of being ostracized, judged, or rejected. You're not doing this to be liked. You're doing this for yourself, to make adversity *your* advantage, and you are worth it.

If you are sharing to help someone else, stay on that intention. Your vulnerability will open other people's eyes. If you have a message you believe will help others, be the messenger.

Be authentic. If you're sharing a message about adversity or trauma and want it to have an impact on someone, it must be 100 percent authentic. We are spiritual beings living a human experience, and we hunt for authenticity in our connections. We can sniff out the difference between the authentic and the fake as easily as a shark smells blood.

Be patient. It took me a long time, until I was thirty-seven, to be able to say to the world that I was sexually abused. By sharing my story, through writing this book and speaking to people, I continue to evolve into a better version of myself. I'm patient with myself as I pull back the layers of my story one by one. Growing up in High Point, being a black woman on an all-white college campus, forgiving my mother, forgiving myself for my DUI—every experience is a layer I can unpeel and share.

SHARE YOUR STORY IN ACTION

Every generation of people hands something off to the next generation. Jay-Z calls it "extending the runway." Jay-Z has helped take hip-hop to the next level, and he will hand the baton off to someone new, who will do even more with the genre. Steve Jobs extended the runway of innovation. Henry Ford extended the runway of the automobile industry. The Wright brothers literally extended the runway. Nelson Mandela and Martin Luther King extended the servant leadership runway. Young people marching against gun violence are extending the runway.

Everything you are doing right now in pursuit of something greater than yourself is you sharing your story in action. You can share your story in action by marching, by protesting, by creating, by doing something that changes the world and the people around you. Artists, engineers, singers, doctors, whoever—we all have tools and gifts that we can use to carry the baton a little bit farther down the track.

Bring your scars to every battle. Bring everything that hurts. Bring everything that's not going well. Bring everything. In the poem "Our Grandmothers," Maya Angelou says, "I go forth / alone, and stand as ten thousand." I've been drawn to this quote in the past four years especially because I've often been the only black woman in rooms full of older white men. At times, I've felt manipulated, disrespected, and mistreated. But every time I walk into one of those rooms, though I come in as one, I am standing on the shoulders of my ancestors, thousands of strong men and women before me who fought and struggled so that I could be in this moment. Understanding this activates my gratitude for all who came before me, and it also inspires me to join their ranks—to carry that baton even further.

Right now, I might be the only black woman in the room, but as I and other black women keep working and marching forward, more and more black women will have their seat at the table. The goal is to have diverse rooms of leadership that represent the people that are being served. I didn't need to march with Martin Luther King; others did that for me. Now my journey is to create my own legacy, where I get to choose my actions.

My responsibility is to speak my truth in order to pave the way for future generations.

I bring my scars to these corporate battles because my scars remind me that I've endured, survived, and even thrived through adversity. I've lost people I loved. I've watched a friend get murdered. I've had a gun held to my head during an attempted robbery right outside my apartment complex. I've been abused. Nothing's going to break me in this moment right now. Nothing's going to happen in this business meeting or in this basketball game or in this interaction with this person that's going to be intense enough to break Adell Harris. If I was capable of breaking, it would have happened by now.

Everything that has happened to me should have broken me; it should have killed me already. But it hasn't. I am an unstoppable force with unlimited potential. Whatever adversity is ahead of me, I say, "Let's go. Good luck."

I encourage you to be an example to others, in action and attitude. Speak on behalf of disenfranchised groups. Speak for the oppressed and marginalized. Stand up to bullying. Show people how to go from victim and villain to hero. Make the assist.

When I started playing basketball at eight years old, I played with my brother and his friends, who were all four and five years older than me. Because of that, I didn't get to play a lot at first. I had to stand on the side and watch. Every time I *was* picked to be on someone's team, it was an opportunity to prove that I could hold my own and be a valuable addition. I couldn't try to shoot the ball every time. My job was to make my teammates look good. It wasn't about me; it was about my teammates. I was picked more and more because the guys knew they could count on me to make the right pass and set them up for open shots. I could make the assist.

I went on to be a point guard, and the thing I loved to do most was assist. My best quality as a basketball player was setting my teammates up and putting them in positions to score easy baskets. I made it look good, too—imagine Jason Kidd, Ticha Penicheiro, Magic Johnson, and Jason "White Chocolate" Williams rolled up into one. As a coach, I continued to make the assist, helping the young women on my teams to become the best players and women they could be.

I'm still making the assist today. That's what I'm doing with this book. I know you have an incredible talent and the potential to do amazing things with your life. My job is to help set you up so that you can make adversity your advantage and achieve your biggest dreams.

SHARE YOUR STORY

We all want to see ourselves in someone else. When we see ourselves reflected in someone else's story, it brings us greater clarity about who we are and what we want. By sharing your story, you can help others get farther along in their journey.

You'll never know the impact you'll have by running your race. You simply have to keep carrying the baton, and one day, you'll look up and realize how much ground you've covered. Then, it will be time for you to pass the baton on. That's how we progress as a society and as a world—with individuals exactly like you pushing forward in order to give future generations a head start.

CONCLUSION

AMOR FATI

In Martin Luther King's final speech, "I've Been to the Mountaintop," on April 3, 1968, the day before he was assassinated in Memphis, Tennessee, he said, "Only when it is dark enough can you see the stars."

The stars are always there, but you need the darkness to see the light—*only* when it is dark *enough* can you see the stars. Dr. King was prophetic in his final speech, my favorite of all his speeches. He said he'd been to the mountaintop and seen the "promised land," and he encouraged the audience to embrace the dark days of inequality, racism, violence, and injustice, because those days were part of the path to the "promised land." If there were no mountains to climb, no dark days to endure, we would never be able to see the stars or reach our promised land.

Life must have contrast. The law of polarity states that everything is on a continuum and has an opposite. There's good and bad, rich and poor, hot and cold, front and back, top and bottom, inside and outside, pleasure and pain, joy and sorrow. You cannot have one without the other. It is the contrast that creates the two. If you only experience joy, it is no longer joy; it is simply the natural state of things. It is by experiencing the sorrow that you can appreciate the joy. The dark allows you to see the light, and so we must be grateful for the dark.

Amor fati is a Latin phrase that means "a love of fate." *Amor fati* is the culmination of everything in this book. According to the *Oxford English Dictionary*, fate is defined as "the events beyond a person's control, regarded as determined by a supernatural power." *Amor fati* is another way of saying that all the aspects of your journey that were out of your control—all the circumstances, events, and people—were intended for you. It's your path, your race, your fate. Loving your fate—every single thing that has occurred in your life, good and bad—will allow you to maximize the potential of your life. It's not just accepting suffering and loss but *embracing* it. It's becoming one with the entirety of your experience and having gratitude for the journey.

You get to choose how you think. You get to choose how you define fear, failure, and adversity, and you get to choose how you view your experiences. We tend to interpret events based on external forces, such as what our families taught us or what other people expect, but we can decide based on our internal belief system instead. Since our imagination is limitless, we have unlimited control over our stories. In my opinion, there is nothing more empowering than that, because how you choose to see yourself can transform who you become and what you achieve.

AMOR FATI THROUGH THE AGES

Amor fati is not a new idea. Throughout time, philosophers, poets, and visionaries have expressed the importance of loving one's fate, of looking at the events in your life as powerful tools that you can use to manifest great change.

As early as the second century, the philosopher Marcus Aurelius said, "A blazing fire makes flame and brightness out of everything that is thrown into it."

In the nineteenth century, English poet William Ernest Henley expressed the idea in his poem *Invictus*:

Out of the night that covers me,
Black as the pit from pole to pole,
I thank whatever gods may be
For my unconquerable soul.

In the fell clutch of circumstance
I have not winced nor cried aloud.
Under the bludgeonings of chance
My head is bloody, but unbowed.

Beyond this place of wrath and tears
Looms but the Horror of the shade,
And yet the menace of the years
Finds, and shall find me, unafraid.

It matters not how strait the gate,
How charged with punishments the scroll,
I am the master of my fate:
I am the captain of my soul.

Then, in the twentieth century, theologian Reinhold
Niebuhr penned the Serenity Prayer, which is used in
Alcoholics Anonymous: "God grant me the serenity to
accept the things I cannot change, courage to change the
things I can, and the wisdom to know the difference."

Now, in the twenty-first century, I'm saying it too, with
this book.

The concept of *amor fati* has persisted throughout time because it is a basic, fundamental truth. If you learn to love your fate, your adversities will become an incredible well of energy, a source of power and strength.

AMOR FATI AND THE REFUSE-TO-LOSE PROCESS

Amor fati is a way of understanding the refuse-to-lose process and journey.

Acknowledging and accepting your pain is about recognizing your adversities are a part of who you are, a part of your fate.

Then, rewriting your story is about choosing to attach positive meanings to all the adversity you've faced and embracing everything that you are. Everything happens as it should, and it's our job to interpret the events of our lives and attach positive meanings to them.

Modeling others is how you adopt the attitudes and behaviors that will allow you to turn your new story into reality. Models also provide us with hope—hope that we can make adversity our advantage and succeed—and they make us feel less alone. They tell us that it *will* get dark but that we will be able to see the stars and find beauty in the darkness. They tell us that we are the masters of our fate, the captains of our souls.

Taking your G and E vitamins is key to loving your fate. Gratitude helps take you from accepting your pain to appreciating it, and empathy allows you to understand the pain of others, eliminating your personal judgments and expectations.

Stating your cause is how you put your adversity to work for you. You have to identify the dream—the thing that will set your soul on fire. When you state your cause, you can harness the energy of your pain to create goodness in your life and in the world, deepening your appreciation for your fate.

Finally, sharing your story is where you give back. Each time you express your truth, you embrace your fate further and empower others to embark on similar journeys. You carry the baton a little farther in the race to add value to the world.

THE POWER OF *AMOR FATI*

Hopelessness is the scariest place to be. Hopelessness is what kills people. It makes people stop trying, and it produces suicide and violence. Hopeless people live in prisons of limitation and lack, manifesting their sadness and internal traumas as anger and toxic behavior in the external world. Hopelessness grows from untreated adversity and trauma, and it takes hold when we can't find answers, when we don't know what else to do.

Loving your fate instills and strengthens faith, which is the opposite of hopelessness. When you practice *amor fati*, you place your faith in a greater power. Some people call this greater power God; others call it the universe or the self. Whatever you call it, a greater power inherently resides within you. It's *your* power, and it is greater than you can imagine; you simply need to have faith in it. Activate the hero inside of you. Activate your gifts, your strength, your wisdom, your confidence, your ambition, and your intuition. You are the magic. You are the power.

Coincidence has come to mean something that is random or happenstance, but I don't believe that. While speaking with a group of college students, one of them said, "Coincidence is the language of the heavens." I love that. In a similar vein, Wayne Dyer pointed out that the word *coincidence* comes from the word *coincide*, which means two things are fitting perfectly together. The coincidences of your life are not random; they are a part of your fate, and they are occurring exactly as they should, as predetermined by the universe. And so, *amor fati* is about working hand in hand with the universe to create the life you want.

Amor fati also gives you faith in your cause. Everything in your life has happened for a reason, for a *purpose*. That purpose is your cause. Everything has been leading to you fulfilling your cause, so how could you not have faith in that cause and in your power to achieve it?

As Marcus Aurelius said, "A blazing fire makes flame and brightness out of everything that is thrown into it." You are a blazing fire. Every aspect of your journey has been fuel feeding your flames. Every disappointment, every hurt, every tear has made you burn all the brighter. By using your adversities as fuel, you make "flame and brightness" out of them.

Loving your fate becomes a source of power in mind and spirit. There's nothing greater than knowing who you are and knowing that everything in your life serves a purpose.

Author Robert Greene describes *amor fati* as "a power... so immense that it's almost hard to fathom. You feel that everything happens for a purpose, and that it is up to you to make this purpose something positive and active." That is making adversity your advantage, in a nutshell.

REFUSE TO LOSE

By embracing all of who you are and practicing the seven refuse-to-lose steps, you can learn to make past and future adversity your advantage. You can, and you *will*. Because the alternative is hopelessness.

It's going to take time and effort, but you are worth it. And luckily, time and effort are both resources we are all blessed with. Sometimes, that's all you have: the time and will to improve yourself every day, to become a little bit stronger, a little bit wiser, a little bit closer to your best self.

Refusing to lose is a continual journey. You can't refuse to lose one time and expect to be transformed for the rest of your life. Refusing to lose must be a lifestyle, a part of who you are. Remember, though, that change is a process. Growth tends to occur in spurts, and it is normal and expected to occasionally face setbacks. Be kind with yourself when you slip back into old paradigms. You may be trying to undo beliefs that have been implanted in your subconscious for your entire life. Just keep working on moving forward. With repetition, the refuse-to-lose process will become more and more like second nature.

When you refuse to lose and lean into the universe's plan for you, you unlock unimaginable power. You become a co-creator with the universe, which is the strongest force that exists. You release guilt, shame, hatred, and anger. You forgive people instead of complaining, blaming, and defending. You become the hero instead of the villain or victim.

I challenge you to not remain at the mercy of your self-destructive behaviors and attitudes. I challenge you to break free of the prison built from the circumstances, events, and people of your past. I challenge you to roll up your sleeves and get to work on how incredible you are. Your most important responsibility is to continue to uncover your greatness every single day, so that you can leave the world a better place than when you found it. Wake up every day and fight to become the person you want to be—the person you are *meant* to be. Refuse to accept limitation. Refuse to let pain control your life. Refuse to lose.

APPENDIX

GRATITUDE LIST EXAMPLE

The following is an example gratitude list, condensed and adapted from my personal gratitude prayer, to help you get started on your own list of gratitudes.

I am thankful for...

- this new day
- this new opportunity
- the moments in the valley
- the spirit of productivity
- every dream and promise in my heart
- all the lessons I've learned along the way
- moments of joy
- my smile

- my confidence
- my resilience
- my family
- financial independence
- the clothes on my back
- the roof over my head
- the vehicle I drive
- the manifestation of my desired outcomes

I *believe* these things to be true, I expect abundance in my life, and I receive these things *now*.

ADDITIONAL RESOURCES
BOOKS

- *7 Habits of Highly Effective People* by Stephen Covey
- *The Master Key System* by Charles Haanel
- *The Seat of the Soul* by Gary Zukav
- *The Secret* by Rhonda Byrnes
- *Think and Grow Rich* by Napoleon Hill
- *The Autobiography of Martin Luther King, Jr.*, edited by Clayborne Carson
- *Awareness* by Neville Goddard
- *Awaken the Giant Within* by Tony Robbins
- *The Four Agreements* by Don Miguel Ruiz
- *The Magic of Thinking Big* by Dr. David Schwartz
- *As a Man Thinketh* by James Allen
- *Lead the Field* by Earl Nightingale

- *How to Win Friends and Influence People* by Dale Carnegie

VIDEOS

- Les Brown, "You Gotta Be Hungry," https://youtu.be/SDIE_QPOPzo
- Les Brown, "It's Not Over until You Win," https://youtu.be/KlUMrzwmbyo
- Les Brown, "It's Possible," https://youtu.be/gXuSMjrx_e8
- Oprah Winfrey, Academy of Achievement interview, February 21, 1991, http://www.achievement.org/video/oprah-winfrey/
- Oprah Winfrey, interview by Barbara Walters, *Interviews of a Lifetime*, 1988, https://youtu.be/V2aACBbXqBM
- Oprah Winfrey, interview by Mike Wallace, *60 Minutes*, December 14, 1986, https://youtu.be/n1NftcOkgic
- Jim Rohn, "Use Your Own Mind, Think, and Make Good Decisions," https://youtu.be/3BDx1t64iXw
- Jim Rohn, "Personal Development," https://youtu.be/jnBdNkkceZw
- Earl Nightingale, "The Strangest Secret," https://youtu.be/EFhkdzj-x8o
- Sylvester Stallone, "Sylvester Stallone on *Rocky*," A Three Legged Cat Production for MGM Home Video, https://youtu.be/sgi3L1z8zBo

- Sylvester Stallone, interview by Brian Linehan, *City Lights*, 1977, https://youtu.be/BoFYdFv43bY
- Sylvester Stallone, interviews by Barbara Walters, *Interviews of a Lifetime*, 1979 and 1988, https://youtu.be/x409m2bGZ4Y
- Tony Robbins, "The Meaning of Communication," https://youtu.be/ruApkmEkPxM
- George Pratt, interview by Larry King, "The Power of the Brain," *Larry King Live*, October 9, 2010, https://youtu.be/WspIpEMotcE
- George Pratt, interview by David Laroche, "How to Enhance Your Life and Overcome Difficulties," 2014, https://youtu.be/11t8h3cIIkk
- Wayne Dyer, interview by Oprah Winfrey, "The Wisdom of the Tao," *Soul Series*, 2008, https://youtu.be/V4zhQ3M892E
- Bob Proctor, "Paradigm Shift," https://youtu.be/z2IEiYM_iYM
- Bob Proctor, "How to Change a Paradigm," https://youtu.be/IOn3AyoUiio

Me with my mother, Joretta Allen Harris, and my brother, Jamel,
Christmas 1985

Me and my brother, Jamel, Christmas 1985

Me and my brother, Jamel, 2013

Me and my first love, my grandmother, Willie Francis, 1986

Me and my first love, my grandmother, Willie Francis, 1988

My best friend, Montre, fall 1997, a few months after his motorcycle accident and just months before he committed suicide in April 1998

Me playing as point guard for Wake Forest University against the University of North Carolina, 2000

Me playing as point guard for Wake Forest University against Duke University, 2001

Me with my mentor, Dana Conte, 1998

Me with my mentor, Dana Conte, 2018

Me with Mike and Marcia McDowell, 2005

Me with Marcia McDowell at Heather McDowell's wedding, 2005

Me with a NCAA Division II regional championship trophy as a first-year head coach at Tusculum College, 2010, thirteen months after my DUI

Me and my mother on our last day together, May 26, 2014 (Memorial Day), one week before she passed away on June 2, 2014. She was more alive than she had been in months, eating, singing, dancing, and wanting to be outside all day. It was a great, happy day for both of us.